GOLDFISH

This red and white Ryukin is an excellent example of the variety; note the over-all elegance and appeal of the fish.

Dedication

To my wife Sheri and to my children Troy, Michelle, Amy and Jessica, whose patience and understanding gave me the opportunity to follow my heart's desires.

A Special Thanks

To Fred Rosenzweig, whose dedication, hard work and superb goldfish photography has done a great deal to increase the interest in fancy goldfish culture.

GOLDFISH

Robert Mertlich

Photography:
Dr. Herbert R. Axelrod; Tom Caravaglia; Jaroslav Elias; Michael Gilroy; C.O. Masters; Robert Mertlich; Compliments of Ozark Fisheries; Fred Rosenzweig; Andre Roth; and Midori Shobo.
Humorous drawings by Andrew Prendimano.

ENDPAPERS: A beautiful pearl-scale Oranda.

Contents

About the Author

Robert Mertlich started spawning and raising fish at the age of 10 when he started raising bettas for the retail market. In his 29 years as a hobbyist he has spawned 70 egglaying species and every common livebearer available.

Robert began his goldfish collection in 1970 and spawned his first goldfish (Redcap Oranda) in 1972. His goldfish spawning activities are limited to rare American and Asian goldfish varieties; during the spawning season he has 45 aquariums in active service raising the fry of these rare varieties.

He has served as a member of the Board of Directors and as Chairman of the Goldfish Society of America.

Introduction

Have you ever walked into your local pet shop and wondered why the price of goldfish can vary more than a thousandfold from a small common goldfish to, say, a fully developed near-perfect Black Oranda or Black Lionhead? After all, a goldfish is a goldfish, isn't it? Well, it is true that all cultivated goldfish belong to the same species (*Carassius auratus*), but today's goldfish are man-made variations of the original wild form, and they vary in many ways—price included.

The goldfish has a longer continuous history as an aquarium fish than any other species of fish. During this long history (well over 1,000 years) the patient hands of Asian goldfish hobbyists have shaped the goldfish into hundreds of different varieties that look nothing like the fish from which they were descended.

The goldfish was developed initially in three areas of Asia: northern China, with its definite four-season (warm to very cold) temperate climate; southern China, which includes areas having a semi-tropical climate; and the tropical Southeast Asia area (Thailand, Malaysia, etc.). All of these areas played an important part in the development of the many goldfish varieties that are the base stock for the goldfish available today.

Many of the rare (and sometimes expensive) Asian goldfish that we see occasionally in our local pet shops are generally raised by one or two small family hatcheries as a hobby/business. In many cases

A common goldfish at five months after hatching. Like any other cyprinid fish it has two paired fins (pectoral and pelvic) and three unpaired fins (dorsal, caudal, and anal).

Introduction

these rare goldfish varieties have been handed down for generations and are a very big part of these families' daily lives and heritage. The total yearly output of many of these rare goldfish is fairly low by world standards, and the fact that fancy goldfish in general spawn very low percentages of quality offspring keep the price of rare or high quality fancy goldfish fairly high when you consider that there is a big demand for them.

There is an old Chinese saying that states, "There is only one good goldfish in each spawn." Boy, I wish that were true, as many times my breeders will give me nothing but junk, and I would have been happy to get even one good fish. But then once in awhile I'll have some spawners that will produce dozens of real beauties in every spawn. Generally rare goldfish are rare even for the breeder of these rare breeds, so if you run across one of these rare—and usually expensive—fish it would be wise to enjoy it as best as you can, because it may be many years before you see another like it again.

Luckily, many fancy goldfish varieties like the Ryukin, Ranchu, Telescope, Fringetail and the ever-popular Oranda breed fairly true to type by goldfish standards and are produced in large quantities, which keeps their prices very reasonable.

For the novice hobbyist, and even for the experienced goldfish hobbyist, the goldfish offers a wide variety of selections and cultivation options to make keeping goldfish a successful, challenging and enjoyable life-long experience. Hobbyists can select those hardy single-tailed varieties that offer easy keeping and lots of activity, or they can select rare, challenging-to-keep goldfish that offer unique beauty and a slow, graceful swimming manner. Add to these varied reasons the long life of many goldfish varieties and it means that goldfish can offer years of beauty and joy to their caretakers.

I'm of the opinion that many English-speaking hobbyists are just starting to learn why Asian hobbyists have spent generations in goldfish culture. Many American and European goldfish hobbyists have begun to realize that there is nothing common about beautiful goldfish and are willing to devote the time and energy necessary to keep these uniquely attractive fish healthy. A hobbyist who spends the time needed to learn about the care of fancy goldfish will have his efforts repaid many times over, as a well cared for fancy goldfish can provide many years of peaceful enjoyment.

It is my hope that this book will help those interested in keeping fancy goldfish to do so successfully so that they too can enjoy the beauty, grace and charm of the grand-daddy of all domesticated fish.

Facing page: A well known fancy goldfish called the Lionhead has no dorsal fin and it also has a mass of headgrowth whose location is comparable to a lion's mane.

General Care

Goldfish are not tropical fish; they are cool-water fish, and they live by a different set of rules that the average tropical fish hobbyist is not used to. Ignore these basic rules and you will have nothing but problems with your fancy goldfish. Follow them and your fancy goldfish will live a long, healthy, active life and will give you much enjoyment as you watch them develop and grow through the years.

This chapter on general care will try to give you a basic understanding of the needs of the cool-water goldfish. Since every aquarium and pond is different, it is impossible to give 100% hard and fast rules for goldfish care. But given the basics and a little common sense, you should be successful in raising goldfish, as they are adaptable to a wide variety of environments.

Life Cycle of Goldfish

The goldfish, in contrast to many other fish available to hobbyists, can be considered to be long-lived. Some of the single-tailed breeds (Comets, Commons, etc.) can live 20 years or longer.

I've been enjoying a Comet in a small lake at a local amusement park for 29 years. Even at that age he shows no signs of slowing down, and he competes very well with his common carp companions for popcorn and trout chow that the patrons of the amusement park feed them.

The fancy double-tailed goldfish are not nearly as long-lived as their single-tailed brothers, but they can and do live for well over 10 years. One nice feature for the fancy goldfish hobbyist is that fancy goldfish improve with age. A goldfish isn't really considered

A common goldfish can be found in red, red and white and calico colors, All of these are excellent goldfish for an ornamental pond or a large aquarium.

Calico Orandas, even from the same spawn, can exhibit a great deal of variability in coloration and pattern as shown by these two fish.

an adult until it's two years old, and these young adults should continue to develop their breed characteristics (such as head growth, color and eyes) every year.

For the first two months of a fancy goldfish's life it's considered a fry and looks nothing like the adult goldfish. Its color is usually olive green, it has short fins, and its one purpose in life is to eat and grow. The goldfish is a seasonal fish by nature and must eat and grow during the warm months if it is to survive the cold of winter. Given enough room, good water and lots of food a fancy goldfish fry can reach the length of two inches or more its first season (spring to autumn). The reason for this fast growth is that the goldfish must be large enough to go through a period of winter hibernation where food is scarce or unavailable.

At the end of two months the well fed, well-cared-for fancy goldfish fry will be half an inch to one inch in length and will possibly have started to develop some of its breed characteristics. It will start to change color and grow fuller in body, and in the eye-type goldfish breeds the eyes may start to develop.

For the first year of a goldfish's life most of the development will go into body growth. Most of the immature (under one year of age) goldfish that are available at your local pet shop will have finnage that is fairly short when compared to the body length. A wise hobbyist takes this into consideration when purchasing a fancy goldfish and doesn't reject a nice young fish because its finnage may seem too short.

A goldfish is sexually mature at one year of age, although

Two fancy varieties of goldfish, an Oranda above and a Bubble Eye below. Both individuals are also double-tailed.

some goldfish that are kept in mild climates will spawn at 9 months of age. As a result of the slow development of many fancy goldfish breed characteristics, many goldfish hobbyists wait until their fish are two years old before spawning them. This wait allows the hobbyist to judge whether items like body, finnage, head growth, eyes and other breed characteristics have developed properly.

A goldfish will continue to develop, grow and (hopefully) improve as it gets older. These large (up to 10 inches), highly developed adult fancy goldfish are only seldom seen in the average pet shop, as they travel poorly and are usually very expensive. Therefore, most hobbyists buy inexpensive immature goldfish and enjoy the excitement of watching their fish grow and develop their adult breed characteristics. The adult breed characteristics of many fancy goldfish do not develop automatically and must be encouraged by using the correct food, maintaining good water quality and by using the correct type of housing for each goldfish breed.

For the most part the life cycle of the fancy goldfish follows that of its ancient single-tailed ancestor. Fancy goldfish are not quite so hardy as their wild relative, but given a modest amount of extra care they will grow and thrive for the pleasure of the goldfish hobbyist.

Surface Area
Because of their large size (up to 20 inches for a single-tailed breed and to 10 inches for a double-tailed breed), goldfish consume a great deal of oxygen. Oxygen enters the water at the water's surface, and the gaseous waste carbon dioxide leaves the water at the water's surface. To make sure there is adequate oxygen in the water the fancy goldfish hobbyist should look for aquariums that provide a large surface area.

Many of the aquariums built today fall into two basic types, talls and longs. The long types are by far the best for goldfish, as they offer more surface area for every gallon of water they contain. For good health a fancy

Any room will certainly be enhanced by the addition of an aquarium with goldfish. However, such an aquarium should be maintained regularly to preserve its good looks and to provide the optimum environment for the goldfish.

goldfish needs, at a water temperature of 70 degrees, 30 square inches of surface area for every inch of body length. If the water is warmer than 70°F it will contain less oxygen than cooler water, so the total number of square inches of surface area needs to be increased for every inch of goldfish in tanks maintained at above 70°F.

To figure the number of fish your aquarium can hold simply multiply its length by its width, and divide this total by 30 to get the number of inches of goldfish your aquarium can hold. As an example, say your aquarium is 12 inches wide by 36 inches long. By multiplying the length by the width you get 432 square inches of surface area. Dividing 432 by 30 will give you approximately 14 inches of goldfish (body length does not include tail fin).

Remember that goldfish are fast growers and allow for this growth when figuring your aquarium's goldfish capacity. Also keep in mind that as your fancy goldfish become older they usually develop a great deal of bulk in their bodies. This bulk needs to be considered, and the wise hobbyist gives large, expensive high-quality or rare goldfish some extra room just in case.

Although this rule of 30 square inches of surface area per inch of goldfish is a very good guide, don't rely on it completely. Many factors can reduce the number of fish an aquarium can hold. As already mentioned, warmer water has less dissolved oxygen

in it, and a great deal of care needs to be exercised to prevent overcrowding during the warm summer months. A heavily planted aquarium or one with dark green water can have its oxygen reduced at night, as plants will consume oxygen during periods of low light, such as on cloudy days and at night. Decaying plants, fish wastes and food can consume a great deal of oxygen, and the hobbyist needs to keep a careful eye on all of these conditions.

Because of their large size and high oxygen consumption goldfish **must not be crowded**. The hobbyist needs to be aware that crowding affects all the fish in the aquarium and can cause widespread disease outbreaks, unwillingness to spawn or other damage to a goldfish collection. Every effort should be made to keep the aquarium a little bit underpopulated to allow for growth and those long hot summer days.

Temperature
Although goldfish can live in a temperature range of 32 to 90°F, all fish have an *ideal* temperature range that they grow and thrive best in, and the goldfish is no exception. Usually this ideal range is the range in which they spawn, and for goldfish this temperature range is in the 60's to low 70's. Most goldfish hobbyists consider 65 to 72°F to be the ideal temperature for most of the year, and I agree. Within that range goldfish are heavy eaters, and they grow well and spawn readily.

A small container, even with aeration provided, is not recommended for keeping goldfish, including the common and hardy kind.

Goldfish's appetites are directly related to the water temperature in which they are maintained. Within a range of 32 to 45°F the fish go into hibernation and really don't need to be fed. A goldfish can go as long as 3 or 4 months without any food—if it was well conditioned with adequate food and was in good health before going into hibernation.

Cold water hibernation is a stressful time for goldfish, and the hobbyist should make a special effort to maintain good water quality during hibernation. Any filtration system used in the hibernation container should not create anything but the most gentle current, as the inactive hibernating goldfish is in no condition to fight heavy water currents. One of the best ways to maintain good water quality in a small hibernation container (under 100 gallons) is a large box filter filled with fresh filter carbon. Do not feed once the temperature drops below 45 degrees.

Goldfish that are in hibernation should be disturbed as little as possible, as any needless activity can cause them to use up their precious food reserves and lower their resistance to diseases.

When the water warms into the 45° to 55F° range a light feeding twice a week, to one light feeding a day, will be enough to keep the goldfish healthy. With a temperature of 55° to 75° a moderate amount of food once to three times a day will meet their needs. Once the water temperature goes over 75° the appetite of the goldfish will start to decrease as there is less oxygen in their water, which reduces their metabolism.

Although goldfish can be kept in a wide range of temperatures, they do best when kept at 65 to 72F° for most of the year. Every effort should be made to keep the water temperature below 75F°, as our golden fish is not happy at warmer temperatures.

Eating Behavior
It has been said that the goldfish is one mean eating machine. And it's true! In my 29 years of raising fish I've never come across a fish which could eat non-stop like the goldfish. It took me a few years to figure out why goldfish are such heavy eaters, but once I figured it out it made perfectly good sense. You see, goldfish are a temperate climate fish and in a natural environment they have to eat a great deal in order to store enough food reserves (fats) in their bodies to last them during the cold water hibernation period of winter, when food is not available.

This eating to excess has caused many home aquarists a great deal of frustration and lost fish. In a natural environment the stored body fats of a goldfish are used up every winter during hibernation, but in the home aquarium, the water temperature usually stays well above 50F° and the goldfish will continue to eat. This continued eating and continued storing of fat by the goldfish will lead to an obese goldfish, and in 2 to 3 years an

Shown here is a Japanese breed of goldfish called Ranchu. It has no dorsal fin and it has a headgrowth like a Lionhead goldfish. The Ranchu is a distinct breed from the Lionhead.

obese goldfish will usually lead to a dead goldfish.

There are three basic ways for the home aquarists to keep their fish from getting too fat. The first is to feed them just enough every day to meet their daily bodily needs. I'll be the first to admit that I find this method impossible and every October I end up with fish so fat that you can see the stored fat bulging along their backs, between their head and the dorsal fin. I'm sure that I'm not the only one who can't resist feeding their goldfish too often, as goldfish are always begging for food. Besides, I've found if you don't feed a bit of excess every day the short round bodied goldfish breeds don't fill out like they should, and look

An alternative to a permanent garden pond for keeping goldfish is a very large earthenware basin. Such a container can easily be moved indoors during the wintertime.

much too lean and long.

So what to do . . .? That leads to the second method of weight control, hibernation. With this method the goldfish is placed in an area such as an unheated basement or garage where the water temperature slowly drops into the 45F° range or lower (32F° is the lowest of course, or you'll have a frozen fish.) I try to keep my fish in hibernation for two months during the winter, which gives them time to use up most of their stored fats.

For many hobbyists this type of cold water hibernation is impossible for various reasons, which leads us to the third method of weight control. For most, this method is the easiest and not only works well in weight control, but it seems to stimulate the spawning urge just as well as a period of cold water hibernation, when followed up by a high protein food conditioning period.

For this method, just feed your goldfish very lightly once every other day for 4 to 6 weeks during the coldest time of the year. For most home aquarists this means during the winter when the aquarium's water is usually in the low 60's. Using this method your fish will probably still slowly grow, but it will do so by using its stored fats.

The reason you just don't want to stop feeding al- together is because at these warm water temperatures the goldfish metabolism will still be very high, and they will need some supplemental food to maintain the necessary vitamins, minerals and other elements for a balanced diet.

For most goldfish a once yearly diet will keep them from getting too fat, and will keep them healthy for a long active life.

While on the subject of good eating behavior, the diet of a goldfish is just a little different from most aquarium fish. The goldfish is an omnivorous fish, eating both plant and animal foods. Many fish foods on the retail market are much too high in protein for the goldfish, and so the goldfish hobbyist needs to either supplement the goldfishes' diet with vegetable foods, or shop for a basic food with a protein content of 20% to 30% and a carbohydrate content of 40% or more.

This basic food will have enough protein for good growth and will be more than adequate for most of the year. If you have spawning in mind, then for the spawning season a food with a protein content of 40% to 50% will allow for a healthy spawn.

Carbohydrates are an important food source for goldfish and should not be overlooked. Not only is this type

If you decide to collect live food from natural habitats you should have some basic collecting equipment, such as a dip net, holding vessels (glass, plastic, or metal), and a set of sieves for sorting.

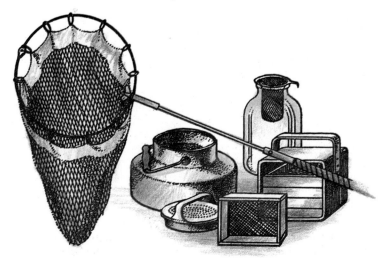

Enlarged image of a live male brine shrimp showing 11 pairs of thoracic appendages and a much enlarged second pair of antennae used as a clasper during mating.

Foods

With the exception of good water quality, the food you feed your goldfish is one of the most important items to successful goldfish culture. Since goldfish will eat just about anything, the feeding of goldfish is not a problem, but for the long life and good health of the goldfish the hobbyist must feed a balanced and varied diet, and do so in moderation.

This chapter on foods will be divided into 3 groups; live foods, commercial prepared foods, and homemade prepared foods.

Since there is no one perfect food I will try to list the pros and cons of each food. The hobbyist should try to feed a varied diet

of nourishment easy for the goldfish's extra long intestines to digest, it also contains a good deal of roughage which aids in digestion. A carbohydrate rich food also helps fill in and round out the bodies of goldfish with short round bodies. It is also useful in intensifying the blue and black pigment (actually blue and black are the same pigments, it's just that this pigment is located in different areas of the scale,) and so it is important in maintaining a good black color on Moors, Black Orandas, Bubble-eyes and Lionheads, as well as to maintain good bright colors in the Calico breeds.

Keep freezedried brine shrimp completely dry and away from dampness. Dampness leads to the formation of mold, and certain species of mold are harmful, sometimes fatal, to fish.

by feeding several different types of food to insure the goldfish get a balanced diet.

Live Foods: *Redworms (earthworms):* This small tender earthworm is right at the top of my list for conditioning goldfish for spawning. Small worms can be fed whole to large adult goldfish, or they can be frozen and chopped into bite size pieces for smaller goldfish.

The short–bodied fancy female goldfish needs a good protein source to develop high quality eggs during the spawning season. But sometimes as she fills with eggs she becomes subject to egg binding and constipation, so her diet has to be carefully watched.

The redworm is high in protein and it has a mild laxative effect on goldfish. This beneficial combination is great for the female goldfish who is filling with eggs, as it helps to produce high quality eggs while reducing the problems of egg binding and constipation.

Adult Brine Shrimp: These little red to green crustaceans live in salt water, and can be purchased at most large pet shops.

Blood Worms: These are the water dwelling larvae of the chironomus midge fly. They are an excellent food for goldfish, as they are small enough for most goldfish to eat whole. They are high in protein and are easily digested by goldfish. They can be purchased from your local pet shop.

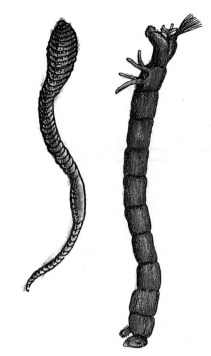

Diagrammatic illustration of an earthworm (left) and a bloodworm (right).

Bloodworms are called such on account of their red color. They are free-living animals and do not feed on blood.

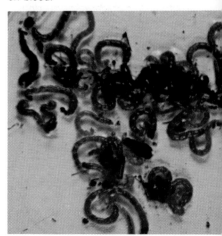

Some fish breeders prefer to culture their own Daphnia *instead of collecting them in the wild. In this way, they are assured of having a supply of uncontaminated food.*

Daphnia: These small crustaceans are another very good live food for goldfish. Sometimes they are known as "water fleas" and include a wide variety of small crustaceans that may or may not be of the same species. They vary in color from red to green to black, depending on the species and the type of food that is available for them to eat. If the water temperature is right (over 68°F,) and there is adequate food, *Daphnia* can be found in very large numbers in fishless bodies of water.

Tubifex Worms: This is one live food I *would not* suggest as a food for goldfish. Due to its polluted environmental habitat, and the high bacteria content of its intestinal tract, it can cause more problems than it's worth. I've even experienced problems with freeze dried tubifex worms, and I now steer clear of all tubifex worm products.

Almost any fish will accept live Tubifex *worms. However, be very cautious in giving them to your goldfish unless you are very certain that they come from an uncontaminated source. They are known to be carriers of parasites of fish.*

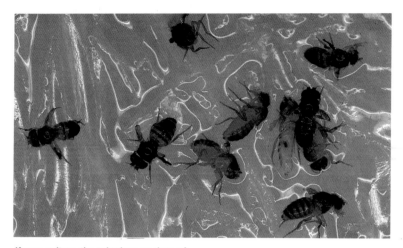

If you culture the wingless variety of Drosophila *you can be sure they are incapable of flying. Having very much reduced or vestigial wings, all they can do is crawl.*

Wingless Fruit Fly: The wingless (*Drosophila*) fruit fly was developed by the scientific community as a tool to help in genetic studies. As luck would have it, for the goldfish hobbyist with a small collection of goldfish these little flies are a wonderful goldfish food. They are easy to culture in small bottles with an inch or so of the agar agar culture medium covering the bottom. The culture medium is somewhat expensive due to the addition of a fungicide that keeps the culture fresh, but for the hobbyist with a small goldfish collection this is a reasonably priced live food. For the hobbyist with a large goldfish collection, feeding fruit flies would take up too much room for the culture bottles, and cost too much to grow to make them practicable.

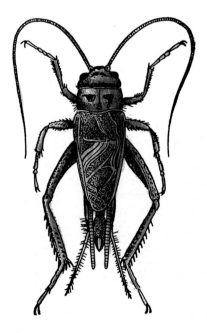

Crickets are abundant at certain times of the year, to the extent of crawling into people's houses. Catch or trap a few and give them to your goldfish.

These maggots are fat and would certainly be acceptable to hungry goldfish. However, certain individuals may find collecting or rearing maggots distasteful.

Insects: Since adult goldfish are large fish they can eat many insects that most fish hobbyists ignore. Small flies, ants, baby crickets, small beetles, grubs, and insect larvae are just a few insects that goldfish can eat. Some of these insects can be cultured (mealworms and crickets,) while others would have to be captured using insect traps or those wonderful electric bug zappers.

Mealworms (not really worms but the larvae of a beetle) are sometimes sold as live food, but they're not among the best live foods for goldfish.

An adult giant mealworm beetle. Beetles that stray into an outdoor pond are eagerly eaten by goldfish. However, certain water beetles can devour goldfish fry also.

Small insects as a goldfish food are hard to beat if the insects are live or freshly killed. They have proven themselves in the pond, as pond raised goldfish usually have better growth rates and color than aquarium raised goldfish.

When feeding insects make sure they have not been in contact with insecticides.

Meal moth larvae are also another insect food that can be cultured with very little fuss at home. Keep your culture covered to prevent adult moths from escaping.

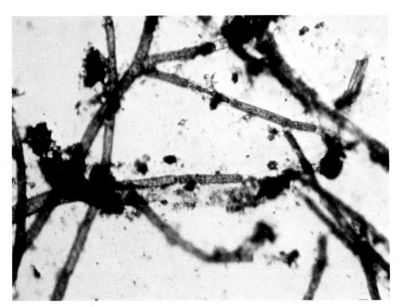

Green algae like Cladophora *can be considered a pest in an aquarium, but a small clump will be consumed by goldfish before it has a chance to reproduce.*

Spirogyra *is a very common green algae present in standing water, ponds and lakes. When seen under magnification, the individual cells are very easy to recognize. Spores are produced by fusion of cellular contents or conjugation as seen on the right.*

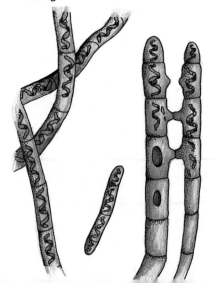

Algae: Goldfish can live on a diet of 90% algae and 10% insects and thrive. Algae is high in protein, has a fair amount of carbohydrates, and is easily digested by goldfish. Not all algae is edible, but fortunately most of it is.

In the pond, algae makes up an important food source for goldfish. For the aquarium goldfish, I'm sure most hobbyists would be outraged at the thought of introducing big chunks of wild gathered algae to their nicely decorated aquariums, I know I would. But if you can overcome your natural inhibition about adding a small amount of algae to your goldfish aquarium, then algae is a good live food source for your goldfish.

The floating plants with the smallest leaves growing in this pool are duckweed, Lemna.

Duckweed and Mosquito Larvae: For those who keep their goldfish in aquariums instead of ponds, this little floating plant is a great substitute for algae in the goldfishes' diet. Goldfish enjoy it so much that you will find it is impossible to grow it in an aquarium that has goldfish in it.

Luckily this is an easy plant to grow, and can be grown very rapidly outside in the sun in a small to large container containing used aquarium water that has had a filter or two cleaned in it. Since this is an ideal container for growing mosquito larvae too, the entire contents of the container should be screened at least once every five days, and the duckweed and mosquito larvae fed to your goldfish. This routine and regular screening should be done to prevent raising a bunch of mosquitos.

To keep the culture producing, harvest only about one half the duckweed each week to feed to your goldfish. The balance should be returned to the culture container with more used aquarium water and the residue left over from cleaning your filters. This routine will keep your duckweed culture producing heavily for months.

Although the life cycle of a mosquito includes larval stages spent in water, the larvae breathe atmospheric air through a respiratory tube near the tail.

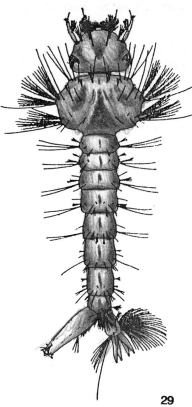

Elodea *is probably one of the common aquatic plant you amy find in your local pet shop. Some species have delicate and tiny leaves; others have a more robust appearance, having broad and more abundant leaves.*

Live Plants: Large adult goldfish eat plants! Keeping this in mind, many of the fast growing plants like *Elodea*, watersprite and other soft and not so soft water plants can be used as a supplemental goldfish food.

To sum up this section on live foods let me state that a balance between live animal and live plant foods are the perfect goldfish foods. Unfortunately due to our large industrial and agricultural economy, many of the natural collecting sites of these live foods are polluted with insecticides, herbicides, industrial and agricultural wastes that makes those natural live foods unfit to use as goldfish foods. Add to this the problem of the possible introduction in your aquariums or ponds of insect pests, diseases or other harmful pests (parasites, hydra, snails, etc.), and many natural live foods can cause a great many problems for the fancy goldfish hobbyist.

If you want to feed natural live foods make sure of the source, and be very careful about screening out any pests before you feed them to your goldfish. For the average hobbyist it is suggested that you grow your own live foods to prevent the damage of feeding a polluted food. In the case of many chemical pollution problems it will take many months or years before a problem becomes visible, and by then it is usually too late to do anything about it. If you are lucky, your pet shop sells live foods!

Frozen brine shrimp are packaged in different sizes, weights, and stages of development—adult brine shrimp intended for grown fish and baby brine shrimp for newly hatched fish.

Frozen Foods: Next to fresh live foods, frozen foods are by far one of the best goldfish foods available. Most of the commercially available frozen foods for fish are too high in protein for goldfish. This isn't really a problem, as you can buy frozen vegetables that can be cooked until tender, and then these can be fed to your goldfish to give them a balanced diet.

On the protein side of a goldfish's diet, frozen foods like blood worms, *Daphnia*, and brine shrimp will furnish their protein needs. Frozen (or fresh) peas (shelled and hulled), spinach, swiss chard, beet tops, carrots, squash, etc., can all be cooked until tender and fed to your goldfish for a balanced diet.

Most pelleted food initially floats on the surface of the water permitting enough time for goldfish to feed before the pellets get water-logged and sink.

Be sure to keep your brine shrimp flakes in a dry place and refrain from shaking the container to reduce breaking up the flakes into dust.

Commercially Prepared Foods:

On the market today are a wealth of some very good, in fact, some really excellent, prepared foods. Unfortunately most are made with the nutritional need of tropical fish in mind, and are too high in protein for goldfish. A good basic prepared goldfish food should have a protein content around 30%, and many of the ingredients should come from plant sources to insure enough carbohydrates and roughage.

Commercially prepared foods come in many different types, but they all have one thing in common, and that is they are all bone dry. Drying fish food makes it easy to handle and inexpensive to package and ship. Unfortunately the large adult fancy short bodied goldfish can have problems eating dry food if the hobbyist misuses it.

The best type of dry food to feed goldfish is the pelleted type. This type comes in many different uniform sizes to meet the needs of different size fish, and has very little dust that can pollute the aquarium. When selecting a pelleted food choose one that sinks rather than floats.

Large adult goldfish are greedy eaters, and in trying to get the most the fastest they will swallow a lot of air. This might mean, in some of the very short bodied goldfish breeds, a goldfish which has difficulty in swimming properly, or worse, a floating fish. This uncontrolled floating usually is self correcting in a day or two, especially if the fish is not fed during this period, but this floating condition does cause a lot of stress to the goldfish as it constantly struggles to swim to the bottom, and this stressful condition is best avoided by feeding a sinking type food.

Another very serious and often fatal problem associated with dry pelleted, or dry ground food is that of intestinal impaction or constipation. This problem is caused when a goldfish (usually a short bodied adult) eats a large amount of dry food very quickly *before* the food has had a chance to absorb enough water. Once this dry food is inside the fish it will absorb the water that is in the intestine, and your prized golden pet is in trouble.

This problem is so easy to avoid it should never happen, as there are at least four good ways to avoid it. The first is to pre-soak the dry food for a short time. If that's a hassle, then try feeding a small amount of dry food several times a day instead of one or two large feedings. If that's impossible, then feed the smallest size dry food that is acceptable for your fish. This will take the goldfish longer to eat and will give the majority of the

Flaked brine shrimp in smaller pieces will be just right for the very young goldfish and small goldfish varieties.

food time to absorb water. The fourth method is impractical for most hobbyists with a small collection of goldfish, and that's not to feed any dry food at all. Of the four methods, I would recommend you pre-soak any dry foods that you feed, as the few minutes it takes to pre-soak can be spent admiring your golden pets.

Flake food, while great for tropicals, is not recommended for large or adult goldfish, as it floats and breaks up into too many small pieces that the larger goldfish will usually ignore. Flake food can be used successfully with small goldfish and goldfish

Goldfish kept in garden pools are usually fed with pelletized food. Feeding them by hand can be a satisfying experience.

fry, as it can be easily broken into small sizes just right for these small goldfish.

Freeze dried foods like bloodworm, brine shrimp and plankton are all good products to feed goldfish for their protein needs, or during the spawning season. Freeze dried foods should be pre-soaked for a short time before feeding to goldfish to prevent intestinal impactions and constipation. Do not soak it too long or it may spoil, and you could harm your goldfish by feeding spoiled food with a high harmful bacterial level.

Homemade Foods: For the goldfish hobbyist with a large collection of goldfish, or for those who want to get more involved in feeding their goldfish, homemade goldfish foods will fill these needs very easily.

GELATIN FOOD FOR FRY AND ADULTS:
1 bottle each, strained baby food, egg yolk, mixed vegetables and chicken
2 small packages Knox unflavored gelatin dissolved in ½ cup cold water
Cold water, enough to bring total ingredients up to 2 cups.

Over medium heat, bring to a light boil. Boil for one minute, stirring constantly (I use a microwave oven and stir twice during the boiling period).

Pour into a container and cool in the refrigerator overnight.

Cut into serving sizes and freeze all but a two day supply which needs to be refrigerated.

Yields two cups of leathery goldfish food. (For adult goldfish you may want to increase the gelatin to three packages for a firmer product.)

GOLDFISH PANCAKES
2 bottles each, strained baby food: chicken and mixed vegetables
4 egg yolks
1 cup white flour
¼ cup whole wheat flour

1 cup milk
1 tablespoon sugar
2 teaspoons baking soda
½ teaspoon salt

Mix all ingredients together very well. Fry using as little cooking oil in the pan as possible (use Teflon pans to avoid using cooking oils).

Make fairly large pancakes and pull them apart into different feeding sizes for your goldfish.

Refrigerate or freeze pancakes to maintain freshness.

BASIC GOLDFISH CAKE
4 tablespoons Spirulina algae (optional)
2 tablespoons sugar
1¾ cups white flour
½ cup corn meal
½ cup whole wheat flour
4 teaspoons baking soda
1 teaspoon salt
3½ cups liquid (1 cup pureed meat—baby food or chicken, turkey, fish, 1 cup pureed vegetables—spinach, swiss chard, squash, carrots, etc., 1 cup liquified eggs, ½ cup milk).

Mix all dry ingredients thoroughly. Add liquid and mix well (you may need to add a little extra liquid).

Pour this very thick batter into two greased bread pans about ½ full.

Bake at 350° for 40 to 60 minutes or until a knife inserted into the center of the loaf comes out clean.

DRY FOODS
Dry foods are made by adding ground or pureed meat, eggs and vegetables to a quick cooking cereal like oatmeal, and then everything is lightly cooked before drying.

A basic recipe would look something like this.
2 lbs. ground or pureed meat and eggs
1 lb. fresh or frozen pureed vegetables
1 lb. cereal mush
Water and salt (follow the directions on the cereal box, figure the meat and vegetables as ½ water.)

Boil lightly for five minutes. (Be careful of splattering.)

Spread very thinly on large cookie sheets and dry in the sun (cover with screen) or a very low oven.

Break into small pieces as soon as possible, and when thoroughly dried grind and sift into various sizes. Freeze all but a two week supply to keep your dry food fresher.

To satisfy a hobbyist's need for greater convenience, frozen brine shrimp is also packaged in a way that individual portions can be popped out of the container instantly.

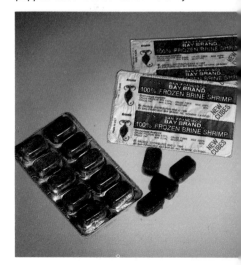

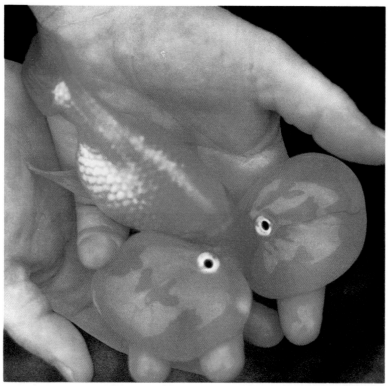

Bubble Eyes are best lifted from the water and moved by hand. This precludes the chance of puncturing the wall of the eye bubbles.

Catching, Moving and Acclimating Goldfish

There's an old story told by some petshop owners that the only way to kill a goldfish is with a gun. This is almost true for that single-tailed common goldfish, but when it comes to some of the very fancy rare goldfish breeds it has been said that even a concerned look can leave them in shock.

Fancy goldfish can be injured very easily by careless handling. Even using a good net can tear fins, remove scales, damage the eyes of Telescopes, rupture the bubbles of Bubble-eyes, and tear off the nasal growths of a Pompom.

Many experienced goldfish hobbyists will use their hands to catch these slow-moving graceful fancy goldfish. The only exception to using your hands to catch fancy goldfish would be the eyed goldfish breeds (Telescopes, Bubble-eyes and Celestials). For these goldfish breeds a small shallow bowl is the preferred catching method, as it avoids causing any damage to these fragile fancy goldfish breeds.

For moving goldfish for short distances, the hobbyist should use a large bowl or bucket partially filled with water from the goldfish's aquarium. Moving goldfish over moderate distances means using a large water-tight plastic bag with a large air space in it, or a two to five gallon bucket with a tight fitting lid and half filled with water. To successfully ship goldfish over long distances taking more than 12 hours, the hobbyist should use large plastic bags with a very large air space filled with pure oxygen. The hobbyist should use two plastic bags, one inside the other, each one sealed separately with a strong rubber band. Ideally the bags should be placed in a styrofoam insulated shipping box or ice chest and firmly secured against movement by packing with crumpled newspaper.

If you are receiving goldfish from a petshop or have received a shipment of goldfish from a distant location, your goldfish needs to be slowly acclimatized to your local water conditions. The best way to do this is to pour your goldfish with the water from the shipping bag into a large bowl or small bucket. Over a period of about one hour slowly add a small amount of water several times from the aquarium to which the goldfish is to be added. Add enough new water to triple the amount of water in the bowl or bucket. The larger or

For long-distance transport of goldfish you may have to request your pet shop to supply you with oxygen. Pet shops also carry the appropriate plastic bags and boxes you need.

Sponge filters are marketed in several styles of construction, but all operate with water flowing through a sponge that traps debris. Sponge filters eventually get clogged and require periodic rinsing.

older the goldfish, the slower should be the acclimating time. This allows these larger fish more time to adjust to the new water temperature and conditions. After this acclimating period, carefully transfer your goldfish into its new home, leaving the bowl and the water it contains.

At this point a word of warning needs to be made. *Never transfer newly acquired goldfish into an established aquarium or pond without a period of quarantine.* Goldfish can and do carry parasites and diseases that could infect all of your other goldfish. Good short-term goldfish quarantine tanks are five gallon buckets, styrofoam shipping boxes, styrofoam ice chests, and heavy shallow cardboard boxes lined with several layers of plastic sheeting. A box or sponge filter will handle the filtration of these quarantine tanks if you feed your fish lightly once a day.

Anatomy

Head: The head of a goldfish is usually narrow and comes to a rounded point in many goldfish breeds. The exception to this are the headgrowth and eye type goldfish breeds. In these breeds the head has been widened between the eyes and the head is almost squarish ending at the mouth in a blunt or squared off fashion. In young headgrowth breeds their head shape is used as a guide for potential future head growth.

Body: The single-tailed breeds have long and slender bodies. There are some body differences in the single-tailed breeds with the Comet being very slim and the Bristol Shubunkin having a slightly shorter and heavier body.

The double-tailed breeds have a wide variety in body shape, from long and slender (Wakins), to short and round (Orandas), to almost ball shaped (Pearlscale.)

Tail fins: The tail fin of a single-tailed goldfish breed consists of one top lobe and one bottom lobe, with a deep fork between these lobes. This single tail fin can be short (London Shubunkin,) long and narrow lobed (Comet) or long and broad lobed (Bristol Shubunkin.)

The double-tailed goldfish breeds have a very wide variety in tail shapes and sizes. Most of these tails consist of four lobes (two top and two bottom) of equal size and shapes, with a fork between the top and bottom lobes. The double tail fins should

Both the Bristol Shubunkin (upper photo) and the Comet (lower photo) are single-tailed goldfish breeds. They are fast swimmers and not too easy to catch in a pond.

be completely separated from each other right to the base of the caudal peduncle. Those double-tailed fish whose tails are partially or totally joined along the top edges are called web tails and are not as desirable as a totally split-tailed goldfish.

Following is a partial list with a short description of some of the basic double-tail fin tail shapes.

Short forked tail fins: Two short side by side tail fins. Found in Lionheads, Ranchus, Wakins, Chinese Pom Poms, etc.

Short square, no fork: A very short delta-shaped tail fin with a squared off trailing end. Found in short-finned Pearlscales.

Fantail: Medium lengthed forked tail fin with medium broad lobes. Found in many breeds but mainly in the Fantail and short-bodied Telescopes.

39

Photographed from the rear the double tail fin of this Pearlscale is very evident. Both halves are similar and completely separated, except at the base of the tail.

Peacock tail: Short forked tail fins held at a right angle to the caudal peduncle. The only goldfish breed to have this type of tail is the Jikin.

Ribbon tail: Long narrow lobes with deep forking. Can be found in many Orandas, Hanufusas (dorsaled pom-poms), and other long tailed goldfish breeds.

Fringetail: Long medium wide lobes with deep forking. Found in Orandas, Bubble Eyes, Celestials, and Fringetails.

Broad Lobe: Long very broad lobes with deep forking. Mainly found in Orandas.

Butterfly tails: Long or short with medium broad lobes and deep forking. When viewed from above the butterfly tail looks like butterfly wings. This is caused by the top two lobes following the curvature of the back and the bottom two lobes spreading at a wide angle from each other. Found in Moors and Lionheads.

Veil tails: Long delta-shaped tail with no forking. Found in long finned Pearlscales and American Veiltails.

Tosa tail: Three broad lobes (webbed), the top two lobes are joined, the bottom two lobes curl and grow in the direction of the head. Found in Tosakins and some Bangkok Moors (very rare breeds.)

Scroll tail: Bottom lobes curled like a scroll. Found in Fringetails and Orandas (very rare breeds.)

Coil tail: All lobes are twisted and curled like watch springs (very, very rare.)

Multi lobes: Having more lobes than four.

There are other types of double-tailed goldfish but these make up the basic types. In every spawn of goldfish you will find a

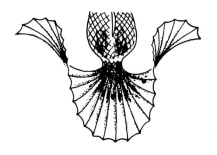

Digrammatic representation of the Tosa tail of a Tosakin.

Dorsal view of a live Tosakin showing the two bottom lobes, each directed to the front, and the large posterior lobe.

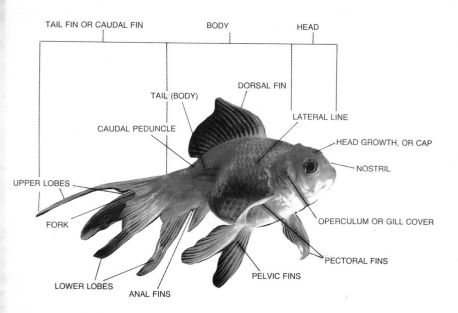

TAIL FIN OR CAUDAL FIN   BODY   HEAD

DORSAL FIN

TAIL (BODY)

LATERAL LINE

CAUDAL PEDUNCLE

HEAD GROWTH, OR CAP

NOSTRIL

UPPER LOBES

FORK

OPERCULUM OR GILL COVER

PECTORAL FINS

LOWER LOBES   PELVIC FINS

ANAL FINS

External anatomy of a fancy goldfish.

wide variety of tail shapes. Some of these tail shapes are pleasing to look at and allow the fish to swim gracefully. There are other shaped tails that are neither pleasing to look at nor allow for graceful movements. It's up to the hobbyist to judge these fine points whenever selecting a fancy goldfish.

Dorsal fin: Some goldfish breeds do not have dorsal fins, but in those breeds that do, they should be held high and erect.

Pelvic fins: All goldfish breeds will have two, and they are long or short, broad or narrow to match the tail fins.

Anal fins: Single tailed goldfish breeds will have one and should be long or short to match the tail fin.

Double tail breeds should have two closely matched anal fins that are long or short to match the tail fins.

Pectoral fins: Two well-matched fins. Long in long finned breeds and short in short-finned breeds.

Dorsal-less breeds: The back contour should form a gentle curve with no bumps, hollows or dorsal spikes in the area where the dorsal fin should be.

To be considered an Oranda, a specimen should have both a well developed dorsal fin and head-growth.

Since this Chinese Lionhead is sexually mature (note breeding tubercles on gill cover and under eye) and lacks much headgrowth, it will not develop enough headgrowth to qualify as a good specimen.

Selecting Goldfish

Many fancy goldfish do not breed true to type in large numbers. For example, a spawn of Orandas will have fish with no head growth to those that have (hopefully) excellent head growths. Add to this, problems with the finnage, color and body shapes and very few Orandas in each spawn will develop into quality goldfish.

If you're in the market for fancy goldfish you should study about the breed of goldfish in which you are interested, and this should allow you to make a good selection in your chosen fancy goldfish breed. If possible, you should try to select from a group of goldfish of the same

breed to allow you to pick and choose and make comparison judgments. Don't rush your decision, as once bought your fancy goldfish will hopefully be around for years.

There are some general items to look for when selecting fancy goldfish, and I will try to explain some of the basic ones.

Headshape: For many goldfish this means a headshape that is narrow and comes to a rounded point at the mouth. On the headgrowth breeds the opposite is true. When viewed from above, the head of an Oranda, Ranchu or Lionhead should be very broad between the eyes, and the head should end at the mouth in an almost squared-off fashion. This broad head will allow room for a well shaped headgrowth.

If you are lucky enough to have found adult goldfish with a well developed headgrowth, try to select those with a symmetrical well balanced headgrowth that will leave the eyes uncovered as the headgrowth develops. A headgrowth type goldfish should have some headgrowth by the time they are six months old or 1½ inches in length. (It won't be much but it should have some.) Protein rich food plays a large part in headgrowth development, but if a headgrowth breed is two inches long, or over a year old and shows little headgrowth development, it should be avoided as in all likelihood it will never have much headgrowth even with abundant high-protein food.

Body Shape: In the single-tail fin breeds the body should be long, thin and in general typically fish-shaped.

The double-tail breeds have shorter and rounder bodies than

A high arch in the contour of the back, similar to a humped back, is very much desired in the Ryukin.

the single-tail breeds. The Fantail has the longest, while the body of the Pearlscale is almost ball-shaped. Most double-tail breeds fall between these two extremes.

It takes about one year for a double-tail breed to fill out, so it is hard to judge the final body shape of a young goldfish. To add to the problem of body shape selection, the final body shape has a lot to do with the care, food and housing the fancy double-tail goldfish has received. The wrong kind of food, and too large a pond or aquarium, will give a round-bodied goldfish a body that is much too long and lean.

An important point to look for in a round-bodied goldfish is the tail portion of the body. This should be be neither long nor too short. It should be broad, thick and strong looking, in order to give the fish the ability to swim properly.

Dorsal-less goldfish breeds should have smooth backs without signs of a dorsal fin,

One of the components of color enhancers sold commercially is carotene, a substance known to enhance color of fish and other animals. Carrots are one source of natural carotene.

hallows or bumps. It's very difficult to find a smooth back on a dorsal-less breed, as only a very small percentage of each spawn will have smooth backs and good body shape.

Fins: The finnage can make or break a fancy goldfish. Look for smooth, undamaged fins without kinks, bends, blood spots, frayed edges or major tears. All paired fins should be well matched. The top and bottom lobes of the tail fin should generally be the same size and shape. In long-fin breeds, all fins should be long; the opposite is true for the short-fin breeds.

Long-finned Pearlscales are a newer variety of the older short-finned breed, and they have become an instant hit with American hobbyists.

A specimen of a Comet with exceptionally long fins.

The tails in double-tail breeds should be split and separated from each other right down to the base of the tail fin.

Young goldfish will have finnage that will appear too short for their body length. The tail, and other fins, usually will start to grow faster than the body during the second year, *after* the body has had a chance to develop its adult shape. The tail and all other fins will usually reach a peak length in relationship to the body during the fourth or fifth year.

Color: All goldfish colors can be improved by giving goldfish some natural sunlight. It's amazing how bright and deep the colors of a goldfish can become in natural sunlight. Many fish sold in pet shops have been exposed to sunlight before they reached these shops, so their colors are bright and deep. Once the hobbyists takes their fish home to the average indoor artificially lit aquarium, these goldfish will start to fade and become lighter in color. This is, unfortunately, natural, and the bright colors can only be brought back by a couple of months of good partial sunshine.

In general, when selecting for color in goldfish, look for bright even coloring. In solid- colored fish (brown, black, orange, blue scale, etc.) the abdomen should ideally have as much color as the rest of the body. In red and white goldfish, the color should be distinct, with red in the majority. In calico breeds, look for lots of sky blue with bright red, jet black and white in a pleasing mix over the rest of the body. The color of the fins in calico breeds, should be mainly limited to black streaks on an otherwise clear fin.

Asymmetry of the fluid-filled eye bubbles is undesirable in the Bubble Eye. Considering the expense and care required, only quality specimens should be purchased.

Eye types: Telescopes and Celestial Eye goldfish should have eyes of the same size, shape and protrude from the head at the same angle. In the case of the Celestial, the eyes should be looking in the same direction (up.) These characteristics are best judged from above, and eyed goldfish breeds should be judged from this angle before purchase.

Bubble-eyes should have large fluid filled bubbles of the same shape, size and attached in the same manner to each eye. Some Bubble eyes will have the eyes in the normal position, while others will have them protruding from the head and looking upwards, each type is acceptable as long as they are the same.

Nasal growth: In the Chinese Pom Pom, Hanafusa (dorsaled pom-pom) and Pom Pom Oranda, the nasal growth should be seen as small ruffled balls at an early age. Pom Poms usually don't start to develop well until the second year.

When selecting any goldfish variety, select those that are active, eating well and are not shy. In other words, those goldfish showing a good deal of vigor. Also, look for healthy fish with few missing scales, uniform fins, clear eyes, no visible signs of disease and clear bright colors. Select the youngest goldfish that fits your needs. Young fish are more adaptable and are usually more hardy. Above all, select those fancy goldfish that appeal to your sense of beauty and for which you're able to fill their environmental needs. This will insure that you will be happy with your pet, and will enjoy many restful hours watching it grow and develop.

Nasal growths that are well separated, similarly developed, are present in this fancy goldfish photographed by Dr. Herbert R. Axelrod.

Brown Pom Pom Telescopes are rare, but well worth the search to find them.

Although this one-year-old metallic orange Pearlscale shows good pearling on the abdomen, it lacks adequate pearling on the back to be considered a good quality fish.

Scale Types

Goldfish have large scales that are usually laid out on the fish's body in neat, overlapping rows. The natural goldfish scale is backed by the crystalline substance *quanine*. This is a very reflective chemical. In the domestic goldfish, the *quanine* has been selectively increased or decreased using genetic modifiers to produce different scale types. The hobbyist should know the difference between these scales.

Many goldfish breeds only have a single type of scale; other varieties may have as many as four types of scales on a single breed. So to make it easy to identify these scales, a list of them follows with a brief description:

Matt: This scale lacks the reflective chemical *quanine* and is, therefore, transparent. The scales are so clear that you have to look very closely just to recognize them. At a distance, matt-scaled goldfish appear to be scaleless. Matt goldfish are usually pale pink in color and have solid black eyes. If they have any color at all it is *usually* just a few spots of black and pale orange. In some highly developed calico breeds, a small portion of the Matts will be brightly colored and are very attractive. Inheritance: Matt to Matt = 100% Matt's.

Metallic: This scale is fully backed with *quanine*, and will appear reflective like the shiny

side of aluminum foil.
Inheritance: Metallic to Metallic
= 100% Metallic.

Brocade: This is a type of metallic scale that has very high levels of *quanine* present. In many cases this type of scale is found in dorsal-less breeds and affects only a few scales along the back. If you look closely at each of these highly reflective scales, in many cases you will probably notice that only a small portion of each scale is affected by this extra *quanine*. There are fully brocaded Orandas on which each scale looked like miniature gold and silver mirrors.

Nacreous: A scale is considered of the nacreous group if it is partially backed with *quanine*. These scales appear to have a soft Mother-of-Pearl sheen and are very attractive. Many calico fish are said to belong to the nacreous scale type class, but in fact most calico breeds have metallic, matt and nacreous scales, and a few have brocaded scales as well. Inheritance: Nacreous to Nacreous = 25% Matt, 50% Nacreous and 25% Metallic. Matt to Metallic = 100% Nacreous. Nacreous to Metallic = 50% Metallic and 50% Nacreous. Nacreous to Matt = 50% Nacreous and 50% Matt.

Spangled: These are metallic scales that appear on a nacreous-scaled fish. As an example: if you have a Calico Oranda with a few metallic scales scattered on its body, it is said to be called a Spangled Calico Oranda. Spangled scales can be brocaded.

This male hi-cap tricolored spangled Oranda has the much sought after solid red cap.

This long-finned Calico Pearlscale shows wonderful coloration and excellent pearling for such a young fish.

Pearlscale: This scale differs from the normal scale in that it has a large, usually white, raised bump in the center of each scale. Pearlscales can be found with matt, metallic and nacreous scales.

Hammerscales: These scales are of irregular size, and the scales don't form neat rows like the normal scale pattern of a goldfish. I've only owned, or for that matter seen one fish with this type scale, but I found it to be attractive as the smaller scales were heavily brocaded and shone like polished gold.

Net-like: This scale is partially backed with *quanine*, giving it a reticulated or net-like pattern. English goldfish hobbyists have worked with this scale for many years, and developed Shubunkin and veils that carry this trait in their genetic make up.

Goldfish Colors
Immature or wild color: light to dark olive green
Gold: orange
Blue: a sky blue to gray blue seen in calicos
Bluescale: sky blue (rare), gray blue, blue black seen with a metallic scale
Red: scarlet to oxblood
Black: coal-black without luster usually over a silver or orange under-color
Ancient Bronze: black to olive with a soft metallic transparent luster
Green: olive green with yellow undertones
Chocolate: a very dark red brown
Mahogany: red brown
Copper: pale red brown
Purple: dark blackish brown with reddish blue undertones

Color Patterns
Calico: blue, black, red and

white on a nacreous goldfish with or without metallic scales

Tri-Color: red, white and black on a nacreous fish with or without metallic scales

Red and White (sarassa): bright red and clear white

Panda: top half of the body, all fins and head black, the abdomen orange to red

Red Cap: the Oranda headgrowth is developed on the top of the head only (hi-cap) and is bright red in color; the body is white

The quality and intensity of colors in goldfish are directly related to genetics, natural sunlight, food, temperature and the health of the goldfish. If the goldfish does not have the genetic make-up for good coloration, then nothing the hobbyist can do will make a big difference in the quality of the color.

Natural sunlight will improve the color of any goldfish. The goldfish should not be exposed to full sunlight all day long and should have a shady spot in the pond to seek refuge. Never expose an aquarium to direct sunlight because the limited water volume will over-heat easily.

A natural green food like algae and some leafy greens will improve the blue and black colors of goldfish. The black pigment is a food storing pigment and a high vegetable diet causes these pigments to enlarge, which darkens the fish. As a side note, the black pigment when found on top of the scale is seen by the eye as jet black. When this same black pigment is located under the scale it can be seen as sky blue to slate gray.

Algae and other foods high in carotenes will improve the red color in goldfish, especially if these fish are exposed to natural sunlight. **A word of warning:** food too high in carotenes may cause the white areas of a goldfish to take on a yellowish cast.

A prolonged period of high temperatures will weaken the color of goldfish. Moors may turn bronzey at temperatures above 70°, but will remain jet

Ryukins, like this beautiful red and white humpback Ryukin, are one of the best fancy goldfish for a beginning goldfish hobbyist to start with, as they are hardy and subject to few problems.

black at lower temperatures (food and genetic make—up permitting).

A goldfish in poor health, or one with a heavy slime coat will have poorer color than it would normally have.

Many factors affect the color of goldfish, and these should be carefully monitored by the hobbyist if bright, deep, rich colors are to be seen on our pets.

Aquarium Companions

Due to the environmental requirements of a fancy goldfish and its gentle nature, fancy goldfish are *not* a good community aquarium fish. Their cool water requirements (60° to 72°) make them unhappy in the typically warmer tropical fish aquarium. The diet of goldfish, and the type of food used to feed them makes it difficult to keep a mixed species aquarium to the benefit of all the inhabitants.

Speaking in general terms, the best companion fish for goldfish are other goldfish. Goldfish are by nature a schooling fish, and are a lot healthier and happier in an aquarium or pond with other goldfish.

Besides, goldfish as a group has more variety within it than almost any other species of fish. So if it's diversity you're looking for, goldfish can give you all the diversity you need. From the fast and active single tail breeds to the slow and graceful double tail breeds; add to this the wide range of colors, scale types, finnage, headgrowth, eye types, nasal growths and those that are

very common and inexpensive, to those that are very rare and expensive, and the goldfish has something to offer every fish—keeping hobbyist.

But, alas, not all goldfish are compatible with all goldfish. Single tail goldfish are very active and move with the speed and agility of most long bodied fish. Add to this the need of large roomy aquariums and ponds so that the single tail finned breeds can develop the length and size that these fish are known for, and you can probably see that these fish are not the best tank mates for the slow-moving double tailed breeds. The short round—bodied double tail fancy goldfish, with its slow graceful motion, needs a small aquarium to develop their short round bodies, and cannot compete for food with the lightning fast single tail breeds.

To divide goldfish up even more, eye type goldfish should not be kept with normal eyed goldfish, as they have poor vision when compared to normal eyed goldfish.

This is not to say that double tailed, single tailed, eye types, headgrowth types and dorsal-less breeds cannot be kept together, as they can especially when young. What it does mean is, if you want to have a better chance of raising fancy goldfish successfully, and to their highest potential, you should try to keep each goldfish breed with other breeds that it can successfully compete with for food and space. In this way each breed will do better and live longer.

A breed like the Bubble Eye requires some thought in the selection of housing and companions. It definitely will be out of place in a garden pool stocked with fully finned and fast-swimming breeds such as common goldfish, Comets, Shubunkins, and others.

Setting up the Goldfish Aquarium

Aquariums and Aquarium Size
One of the first of the Golden Rules the goldfish hobbyist needs to learn is to never, never crowd the golden pets.

Goldfish need lots of oxygen rich water, plenty of growing room and water that is very low in the metabolic waste ammonia to maintain their good health, and to insure them a long life. The easiest way to give your goldfish these three items is by giving your goldfish large aquariums with lots of surface area.

Although a few small immature fancy goldfish under one year of age can be successfully kept for a short time in an aquarium as small as 10 gallons, for the average goldfish hobbyist I would recommend that 20 gallons be the smallest aquarium that should be purchased. This will allow plenty of growing room for three to four fancy goldfish

This fancy aquarium is not recommended for keeping goldfish. The surface area where exchange of respiratory gases takes place is too limited.

for several years.

Because of the many different shapes and designs of aquariums that are available today, the hobbyist should look for those that offer the most surface area for the number of gallons they contain. This usually means that the long aquariums are to be preferred over the tall or hexagon aquariums. Remember the rule of 30 square inches of surface area for every inch of goldfish (body measurement only) and you will have very little trouble meeting the space requirements of goldfish.

Besides the glass aquarium, goldfish can be kept in many different types of containers. It would be impossible to mention them all, but I will list a few to give you an idea of some of the more common ones:

1. For small goldfish (fry to two months) large plastic bowls, large plastic sweater boxes, and styrofoam ice chests.

2. For medium sized goldfish (under one year of age) you can use large styrofoam ice chests, styrofoam fish shipping boxes, childrens' plastic wading pools and, in an emergency, a five gallon bucket will work well.

3. For large goldfish, or a large collection of goldfish, a vinyl lined metal walled circular wading pool works very well. These small pools are six to eight feet in diameter and 18 to 36 inches deep. Many of these pools come complete with sand filters that can be modified into a big canister type filter that really moves the water.

4. Also on the market are pre-cast fiberglass ponds that can be built right into your house, patio, sunporch or yard. With a little thought and planning they can be made to look very natural and attractive and because of the large surface area these ponds offer, your goldfish will do very well in them.

5. For those who want to go all out, the outdoor pond can extend the goldfish habitat to the yard. An outdoor pond can be as complex as a concrete pond, to a hole lined with a vinyl swimming pool liner or heavy plastic sheeting. For those who are interested in pond construction, I would suggest going to the library or visit a local pet shop for a good book or two on pond construction. A well designed pond is a pleasure to have and care for, a poorly designed pond is a nuisance, so do some home work before you get out the old shovel.

Filters

Fancy goldfish are very sensitive to poor water quality, and one of the easiest ways to maintain good water quality is by filtration. For the average hobbyist this means mechanical filters and/or biological filters. Both of these types of filters come in air operated and power models, and each type can be successfully used with goldfish.

Air operated filters work very well in an uncrowded aquarium where the diet (food consumption) of the goldfish is carefully monitored to prevent overfeeding. When selecting a filter that is operated by air, try to select a model operated by an airstone, as these move much more water through the filter than the bubble tube types.

Power filters are used very effectively in large aquariums, or aquariums that are slightly overcrowded (*for shame, but we all do it*). Because they move

A basic undergravel filter will be adequate for a tank with a few goldfish, not recommended for a densely populated tank which needs a faster rate of water flow.

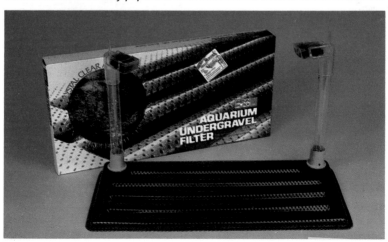

An outside filter, by virtue of being situated out of the water, is more convenient to operate and clean than a submerged box filter that also takes up very much needed space in an aquarium.

many times the amount of water through the filter, they can hold and maintain good water quality even during periods of adverse conditions, like warm water and slight overcrowding. The hobbyist should be warned not to rely too heavily on these filtration monsters and ' overcrowd their aquariums, as even a short power failure can wipe out a goldfish aquarium that is pushed beyond its holding capacity.

Power filters have one main problem in the goldfish aquarium: they create a very strong water current. Fancy round bodied goldfish are not the best of swimmers, and quickly become exhausted when they have to continuously fight strong water currents. When using a power filter try to position the discharge so that at

least one area of the aquarium has little or no direct current from the filter. This will allow your fancy goldfish the opportunity to find a place of refuge where it can rest and regain its strength.

If your power filter has a tube discharge then the water current can be minimized by attaching the discharge tube to a length of perforated rigid plastic tubing. If possible try to attach this perforated tube to the aquarium just above the water line, as the discharge water splashing on the water's surface will increase the oxygen absorbed into the aquarium's water.

Mechanical Filters: This type of filter generally uses a fibrous material to physically remove the solid particulate waste and a carbon or charcoal layer to remove certain liquid and gaseous wastes. On a few mechanical filters an extra chamber is provided that can be filled with very coarse gravel, or preferably bone charcoal, and this chamber can act as a biological filtration chamber. This biological chamber should only be lightly cleaned when it starts to become clogged so as not to disturb the beneficial bacteria.

One of the most commonly used mechanical filters is the inside box filter. Even though they take up room inside the aquarium, they are good work horses and filter a small aquarium fairly well.

For a filter that is easy to care for and is better to use in formally decorated aquariums, the outside filters are the answer. They come in waterfall discharge models, tube discharge, and in the case of the canister filters come with the filter floss and carbon in pre-made, pre-measured units that can be quickly, neatly and easily changed with a minimum of fuss. Other models take bulk floss and carbon and can use a variety of materials. This latter group does take longer to service, but generally they are less expensive to maintain.

Many people ask which is best to use, filter carbon or the less expensive charcoal? The cost of filter *carbon* is well worth the small extra cost, as it lasts much longer and seems to work quicker than *charcoal*. Luckily, carbon and charcoal can be easily reconditioned by placing clean, rinsed, air dried carbon or charcoal in the oven on shallow trays for 45 to 60 minutes at 450°. Just a friendly warning, if you fail to rinse and dry the carbon and or charcoal thoroughly you may be treated to the smell of a well established barn yard coming from your oven.

Biological Filters: To many people biological filtration means the undergravel filter. The undergravel filter uses the gravel in the aquarium to filter particulate or solid wastes from the water. Then within this bed of gravel various bacterial cultures use oxygen from the water to oxidize these wastes into safer chemicals that are not as harmful to goldfish. The air-operated undergravel filter is a fair filter, but it usually is not powerful enough to filter the goldfish aquarium, unless the aquarium is very lightly populated or is populated by goldfish fry.

But thanks to the competitive aquarium supply manufacturers, powerheads that fit on the undergravel exhaust tubes have been made available to the goldfish hobbyist at a reasonable cost. These powerheads increase the flow of water and oxygen through the gravel bed, which increases the efficiency of these undergravel filter tens of times over the air operated models. These powerheads do create strong water currents, so the hobbyist needs to position them in such a way that at least one area of the aquarium stays generally calm.

The installation of a power head can accelerate water movement through an undergravel filter.

Artficially colored gravel may not be desirable to some hobbyists, but it does provide much color to an otherwise drab aquarium.

Because we are dealing with living organisms that do the actual filtering (water purifying) in the undergravel filter, undergravel filters take at least two weeks before they build up enough of these beneficial organisms to start to work with any degree of efficiency. And it will take as long as four weeks before it has reached its full potential.

This period can be speeded up slightly by inoculating the undergravel filter with water and gravel from an established aquarium, or by using one of the commercial products available for starting undergravel filters. In any freshly set up aquarium, fish should be added slowly over a period of two to four weeks, and their diet held to a minimum to give the undergravel filter time to establish, so that it can handle a full biological load.

To sum up this section on filters and their use in the goldfish aquarium or pond, the goldfish hobbyist should use both mechanical and biological filtration methods. This will insure the highest water quality for your goldfish, but do not over-filter your aquariums. A filter that will filter all of the water in the aquarium two to five times every hour is more than enough to keep the aquarium clean. As an example an outside power filter rated at 100 gallons an hour is just right for a twenty to thirty-five gallon aquarium.

Gravel
Many hobbyists prefer to use aquariums with no gravel in them, to house their goldfish. For those who have a large collection of goldfish with many aquariums, this type of gravel-less set up does cut down on maintenance time, and the goldfish do very well in bare bottomed aquariums.

Using this type of habitat means that the undergravel

biological filter cannot be used, so one of the portable biological filters and mechanical filters must be properly maintained to insure good water quality.

For the average beginner in the goldfish hobby the question of what size and what type of gravel is asked more often than "Should I or shouldn't I use gravel?" For the hobbyist who uses gravel, use the best gravel available from the local pet shop rather than gathering your own.

When buying gravel choose the medium coarse smooth gravel. Goldfish are browsers by nature and will take up mouthfuls of gravel, chew on it for a short time and then spit it back out, usually in a spot where you don't need any extra gravel. Since goldfish have a habit of transporting gravel as they chew it, this underwater excavation can move a lot of gravel given enough time. Using the medium coarse sized gravel reduces

gravel moving somewhat, and yet it is not too large to be useless as a cover for your undergravel filters.

The gravel in the goldfish aquarium should be smooth, so as not to injure the fragile mouth of the goldfish on any sharp edges as they chew it, and to make it easy for them to spit it back out. This latter reason is important as goldfish will, from time to time, get small pieces of gravel stuck in their mouths.

If one of your goldfish gets a small piece of gravel stuck in its mouth give it several hours to dislodge it by itself before you do anything. If it fails to dislodge the stone in a reasonable length of time then try turning the stone in the goldfish's mouth with the round end of a flat tooth pick to see if this will allow the fish to spit it out by itself. Be very careful when doing this as the small bones around the mouth of a goldfish are very easily broken.

Having a few pumps of various strengths is not an extravagance. The value of a spare pump for an emergency replacement in case of a breakdown can not be ignored.

Fluorescent tubes of varied sizes and wattages, are available to suit the type of reflector you have. If there are live plants in your tank you should use plant-benefiting tubes.

Light

The natural sunlight found in the well designed outdoor pond has a wonderful effect on the color and well being of a goldfish. If it's possible for the hobbyist to give their goldfish some natural sunlight without the danger of overheating the water, then the hobbyist should make the effort to do so.

For the average hobbyist with an indoor aquarium, there are usually two options for lighting the goldfish aquarium: natural room light or the light from an aquarium reflector. The additional light from the reflector is usually chosen by the hobbyist as this shows off the fish better and allows the hobbyist to grow aquarium plants.

When selecting a reflector, select the slightly more expensive fluorescent light reflector. The amount of heat given off by the fluorescent light is considerably less than incandescent light bulbs, and this helps to keep the water cooler. They are also less costly to operate, the bulbs last longer and by using Grow Lux fluorescent tubes, the color of the goldfish can be enhanced while getting better plant growth. Petshops carry these tubes.

But additional light is really not necessary. Goldfish really don't need any additional light from an aquarium reflector as long as the room they are in is bright enough for you to read in. In fact, if your aquarium is plant-less, it would be wise during the heat of the summer to leave the reflector light off to keep the aquarium cooler during these long hot days.

Air Systems

With an air system for water circulation and filtration an aquarium can hold considerably more goldfish than an aquarium without one.

Most hobbyists use the rubber diaphragmed electric air pumps to run their air systems. These are a great choice as they are inexpensive to operate, easy to repair and there is a size to fit almost everyone's needs.

For those hobbyists who have several tanks that are close together, or for those that have extra large or very deep aquariums, they can purchase a piston type pump which delivers more pressure than diaphragm pumps.

The hobbyist who operates dozens of tanks needs a large air system that can furnish enough air for hatchery tanks, brine shrimp hatcheries, filters, plus a lot extra just in case. Many of these large air systems can be furnished fairly easily by several specialty manufacturers that advertise in tropical fish hobbyist magazines. Or you can look around locally for air sources such as air compressors (an air cleaner and pressure reducer needs to be used), rotary blowers or a late model automotive smog pump connected to an electric motor used as an air supply source (noisy but effective).

No matter what air source you use they are all basically controlled at the aquarium using air valves. Air valves are the weak point of any aquarium air system, as many cheap ones leak, are hard to adjust or restrict the air flow through them. Even some of the more expensive ones have these

faults. In general look for air valves in groups of three to five, that are of the lever type. The lever types are a bit harder to adjust, but they seem to leak less and last longer than those that are threaded with an adjusting screw.

The next problem the hobbyist may experience is noisy airpumps and loss of air pressure. This problem is usually caused by a clogged airstone. Airstones have a limited useful life, and when they get hard to blow through compared with a new one, they should be replaced before they damage the air pump.

Years ago airline tubing used to be expensive, but it remained pliable and was useful for years. Today's airline tubing is very inexpensive and can be discarded and replaced by a new piece when needed, which is a

A gang of well constructed valves is worth the extra cost. Leaks, if neglected too long, reduces the efficient delivery of much needed air.

good thing as it usually will fossilize after a short time in the aquarium.

When buying or planning an air system, the hobbyists should always consider buying the next size larger air source than their immediate needs. This extra air will come in handy if another aquarium is purchased, or when extra air is needed for a quarantine tank or other temporary use.

Remember for longer pump life to bleed all excess air through an empty valve to prevent back pressure from damaging the pump.

Under some circumstances it may be necessary to remove chlorine by chemical treatment. Products that neutralize chlorine are available at pet shops.

Water Treatments

In areas where the community water supply is treated with chlorine all water must be aged for several days or treated with chemicals to make them safe to use. Your local petshop sells "chlorine neutralizers."

If you're unlucky enough (for fish reasons) to live in an area that has the water treated with chloramines (chlorine and ammonia), aging the water will do little good, unless you can do so for 30 days with lots of water circulation. Usually chloramines are treated with chlorine and ammonia neutralizing chemicals, and a day or two of aging makes the water safe for goldfish.

If you live in one of the few areas where the water is not treated with any disinfectants, it should still be aged at least overnight to allow any compressed gases to dissipate; this is especially true of well water.

For small partial water changes (5% or less) water treated with chlorine is generally safe to use directly from the tap, if the gases are allowed to escape and the smell of chlorine is very light. Water treated with chloramine must be treated with chemicals to neutralize this persistent chemical disinfectant as it is a goldfish killer. Remember this if you use automatic water changes.

Interior Decorations

Backgrounds: With the exception of an aquarium that is viewed from both sides, most aquariums look best with an opaque covering on the back of the aquarium.

Hobbyists has a wide selection when choosing a background. They can choose mirrors, custom fit 3-D backs, printed underwater scenes purchased by the foot, color foil, or a colored lacquer that forms crystals as it dries. Most of the commercial

The decor of a tank is a matter of personal taste. The choice is only limited as to whether the item chosen is harmful or not to goldfish.

backgrounds can be applied quickly with just a little clear tape, except for the crystalled lacquer. This lacquer must be applied in a well ventilated room (or better still in the back yard), and cured for several days to get rid of the very noticeable fumes.

Rock: Hard insoluble rocks like flint, agate, some granites, jasper and basalt are all good rocks for the home aquarium. Soft rocks that contain limestone or other soluble minerals (iron, copper, etc.) are not suitable for aquarium use, as these can be toxic to goldfish.

Rocks used in the aquarium should be well worn and reasonably smooth to prevent injury to the aquarium inhabitants.

Ceramic and Plastic Decorator Items: On the retail market are many man-made items from caves to sunken ships to diving dogs that go up and down. If the hobbyist wants to use any of these items, and if these items have no sharp edges, then they are perfectly safe to use with goldfish. Be aware that many items like sea shells, rock, and man-made products are traps for fish wastes and must be cleaned regularly to prevent water pollution.

Setting up the Goldfish Aquarium

Plastic Plants: Plastic aquarium plants have come a long way over the last few years. Some are so real looking that once they are in the aquarium about the only way you can tell them from the real thing is that these plastic imitations are far too perfect looking.

If your aquarium lacks enough light, or your goldfish eat the plants you try to grow, then by all means use plastic plants as they will make the aquarium more attractive and natural looking.

Some artificial rocks and plastic plants are so realistic in appearance that a closer examination is needed to be aware of their being imitations, not the real things.

Driftwood: Some woods are fairly safe to use in the aquarium, but other woods, like redwood, are not safe to use at all. The problem with any dead organic material, and driftwood is one such item, is when it is exposed to water it tends to decay and will slowly change the pH of the water in the aquarium to the acid side of the pH scale.

If you make *regular frequent partial* water changes, wide pH swings are not a problem if your water is neutral or slightly alkaline to start with, so driftwood would be safe to use. But if you fail to make frequent water changes your aquarium water's pH and the pH of the water you use for your water change will be far apart and can cause problems with your fancy goldfish. If the water in your area is already on the acid side then I would not use driftwood, as you may find yourself with water too acid for the good health of goldfish.

If you use driftwood do so with caution, and try to determine if it is a safe wood to use in the aquarium. Make frequent partial water changes a regular part of your fish keeping schedule and keep a careful watch on your pH. Only use driftwood you buy at a petshop as this is usually safe; garden store driftwood is usually unsafe.

Live Plants

Goldfish love plants! In fact goldfish eat plants, and they thrive on them.

Small immature goldfish aren't really much of a threat to your planted aquarium. But put a six to eight inch Oranda or Ranchu in your planted aquarium and all but the toughest plants will suffer.

Some good goldfish plants for the aquarium are Amazon Sword plants, *Cryptocoryne*, Giant *Vallisneria*, all *Sagittaria*, and if the tank is brightly lit then some of the dwarf lilies and spatterdocks will do well.

For the pond many of the aquarium plants can be used (at least during the summer), as well as water lilies. Water lilies are great for the goldfish pond as they provide shade for the pond and fish as well as color in the form of beautiful flowers for the hobbyist. Water lilies should be planted in large pots with the top of the soil covered with coarse gravel to keep the fish out of the soil. There are specialized books on water ponds and water lilies.

Live plants in the aquarium or pond are a lot of work, but a well designed and planted pond or aquarium is beautiful beyond words. If at all possible the hobbyist should try to have at least one planted goldfish habitat, as the work, money and time spent is well worth the effort.

The damage done to plants by goldfish can be held to a minimum by keeping the goldfish well fed (several small daily feeding), and by keeping only small one and two year old goldfish in the planted aquarium.

Heaters

For the average hobbyist, living in the average house, with an average aquarium, in the average room, the aquarium heater is not needed. If for some reason you are not average, and the water temperature in your aquarium stays below 60° for a long period of time, then a heater might be handy to raise the temperature into the 60° range.

A heater is generally a must

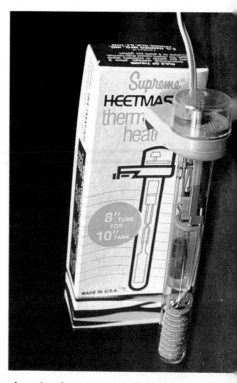

Aquarium heaters are available in two basic types, submergible and non-submergible. Shown is a an ordinary aquarium heater which can not be completely submerged.

for incubating goldfish eggs and raising goldfish fry during the early part of the spawning season. For this use, a submergible heater is the best type to use.

Remember the goldfish is a cool water fish, and a short period of cold water hibernation is a benefit to our golden friend. For most indoor hobbyists an aquarium heater will never be needed, and the money spent for one would better be spent on a powerhead for your undergravel filter.

Ammonia, Nitrites, Nitrates and pH

Goldfish are heavy eaters and they produce a great deal of waste products. Most of the solid wastes can be removed by the mechanical filter. The gaseous wastes (mainly carbon dioxide) are eliminated at the water's surface while oxygen enters the water in the same way. Some of the other toxic water-soluble chemicals are removed by carbon, charcoal or other products that the hobbyist can purchase at the local

Carbon filter cartridges are inexpensive and easy to install and replace. A used cartridge is completely disposable, the carbon particles remaining within the confines of the container.

petshop. But to complicate the keeping of goldfish, there is one toxic goldfish waste product that can be difficult for the hobbyist to control using a mechanical filter and that's *ammonia*.

There are products on the market that absorb ammonia very well, but due to the heavy production of ammonia by a school of goldfish, these products do not last very long. Using them causes the hobbyist two major problems. The first is the hobbyist never knows if the ammonia absorbing product is working or has stopped working. The next is these products are very effective when first installed and will reduce the ammonia to almost zero, but on the next day or the day after the ammonia can reach critical levels. This up and down of the ammonia level causes rapid instability in the water quality which is not healthy for goldfish.

Although long term ammonia control is difficult using the mechanical filter, it is very simple to control for months on end by using the biological filter (undergravel, sponge, etc.).

The bio-filter and its beneficial bed of nitrofying bacteria, uses the oxygen in the water to oxidize ammonia into a nitrite, a somewhat less harmful chemical. The bio-filter, and another group of beneficial bacteria, reduce the nitrites into an *almost* harmless (to fish) chemical called nitrates, which is easily controlled and removed by regular water changes.

A bio-filter is not a cure all, and it needs time to become established (two to four weeks for a newly set up filter). But given a good flow of oxygen rich water through the gravel, the bio-filter can maintain good water quality more dependably than 90% of the mechanical filters on the market. The bio-filter needs to be lightly cleaned regularly to keep the water flowing through it easily, and it can't be exposed to bacteria killing chemicals, such as antibiotics.

You're probably wondering why worry about ammonia, nitrites, and nitrates?

Ammonia is a deadly goldfish killer. It attacks the skin, fins, circulatory system, liver and kidneys of a goldfish. A continued moderate level of ammonia, or a brief seriously high level of ammonia can cause damage or total failure of these bodily systems and organs. Ammonia can be a slow killer and the fish may die weeks after being exposed to high levels of ammonia, or it can kill quickly in just a mattor of a few days.

Signs of ammonia poisoning are rapid breathing, fin congestion, blood spots on the body, and in bad cases, ammonia can burn. This will cause the fins and other body parts to turn black (this blackening can also be caused by some chemicals other than ammonia, and by injuries).

It's impossible to tell you just how much ammonia (ppm) is harmful to goldfish, as pH has a lot to do with the toxicity of ammonia. At a pH below 7.2 ammonia is not as nearly as harmful as when the pH is above 7.2. Also it seems every goldfish has a different tolerance level to ammonia. Some goldfish will succumb to ammonia at very low levels, while some seem to thrive at moderately high ammonia levels.

There are on the market some liquid aquarium ammonia neutralizing chemicals, that when

Always follow the instructions of the manufacturer in the proper use of a water purifier for maximum effect.

added to the water will temporarily neutralize ammonia. All goldfish hobbyists should keep one of these products in their emergency goldfish medical kits for emergencies or when shipping goldfish.

Nitrites are not nearly as damaging to goldfish as ammonia is, but it still can be very deadly. Signs of nitrite poisoning is a goldfish breathing heavily near the surface or in a corner. Nitrites reduce the oxygen carrying ability of the blood, causing a condition known as brown blood. It can be fatal, and is usually a problem for the hobbyist when breaking in a new undergravel filter. The bacteria that convert nitrites into nitrates lag behind those that convert ammonia into nitrites, so there is a brief period when breaking in a new bio-filter that nitrites can be a problem.

The easiest way to keep nitrites from becoming a

problem is to break in a new undergravel or other bio-filter slowly. Populate the newly set up aquarium lightly and feed sparingly, slowly increasing the aquarium's inhabitants and the frequency and amount of food over a four week period.

SAVE FISH LIVES!
FAST — EASY — ACCURATE

wardley's
SENIOR DELUXE
pH TEST KIT
for Aquarium Water

Test for Acidity, Alkalinity or Neutrality of
aquarium water. Insure proper breeding.

A pH kit is necessary for monitoring the aquarium water's pH. Some kits contain testing equipment only, while others contain both testing equipment and water treatment chemicals.

If you suspect high nitrite levels, take immediate action by adding one teaspoon of salt to every five gallons of water. The amount of salt can be increased to three teaspoons per five gallons of water without any harm to the goldfish, plants or other aquarium inhabitants. This amount of salt will usually stop the goldfish from heavy breathing near the surface and corners, and relieve their oxygen distress. A partial water change several hours after the salt treatment is generally beneficial.

Salt will reduce the effectiveness of many ammonia absorbing products, and in fact will usually render them useless.

Nitrates in small amounts are generally considered to be harmless to fish. In large amounts nitrates can weaken the fish to the point of causing the fish to become infected by fungus or bacterial infections. Signs of high levels of nitrates are a heavy slime coat and dull color on a goldfish. A heavy slime coat can also be caused by disease, parasites or other chemical irritants.

Nitrates are easily controlled by frequent partial water changes. Nitrates are also used by plants as food, so thriving plants can help to keep nitrate levels low.

pH: Goldfish do well in a wide range of pH. Any change in pH should be done gradually, especially with eggs and young fry.

A pH between 6.8 and 7.2 is an ideal range, but don't worry too much about pH, just keep it above 6.0 and below 8.0 and you'll have healthy happy goldfish, if other water quality problems are kept under control.

Water Hardness: Goldfish have a wide tolerance to water hardness. Generally if the water is fit to drink, goldfish will do very well in it. Goldfish do seem to do just slightly better in a moderately hard water over soft water.

In any case don't make any changes in your water hardness unless a problem can be directly linked to it. Long term stability is more important than the hardness of the water.

Disease

Since many goldfish diseases look alike, it is sometimes very difficult to determine if a disease is bacterial, fungal, parasite, environmental or genetic in nature. To lessen the stress and problems caused by improper treatment, if you can't readily recognize the disease your goldfish has and before you start dumping all sorts of medications into your aquarium and killing your filters and biological balance, it might be wise to try a partial water change and adding a little salt to your aquarium. Many times this simple treatment is all that is needed to cure your goldfish.

If the disease isn't environmental in nature, then the hobbyists should do their best to determine the exact nature of the disease. An experienced goldfish hobbyist, or a knowledgeable petshop owner should be consulted, if possible. It's very important to treat the disease with the correct medication or you may not be successful in treating your sick fish.

You also should make sure you follow the manufacturers' directions very carefully. If you treat your fish haphazardly with antibiotics and other medications you may develop a disease that is resistant to medication and is therefore untreatable with the medication available to the average hobbyist.

It is better to prevent diseases by isolating new fish, maintaining good water quality, proper food and feeding, correct temperature and by giving your goldfish large uncrowded aquariums. If the goldfish hobbyists learns this, they will usually only have to worry about

This Telescope goldfish is blind, and both the dorsal and caudal fins are fungused. The eye condition is not reversible, although with the appropriate treatment the spread of fungus can be stopped.

Any break through the skin can develop into a festering sore when invaded by bacteria that are normally present in the water. Slight mechanical injuries of the skin should be treated as soon as observed before an infection sets in.

genetic problems, and since these are not all that common the hobbyist should have a pleasant experience in keeping fancy goldfish.

A sick goldfish is fairly easy to recognize. It may be listless, have a poor appetite, clamped fins, poor color, heavy slime coat, cloudy eyes, red spots on fins or body, open sores, poor swimming ability, torn fins, missing scales, fuzzy growths on

Specific remedies for the control of parasites are available in most pet shops.

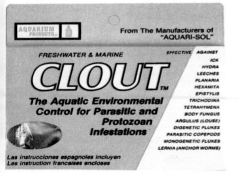
body or fins, parasite infections, or just may not look right.

Quarantine
All goldfish whether bought from friends, breeders, petshops, wholesalers, or importers, should be quarantined from all other fish in your goldfish collection for at least two weeks. The water temperature in the quarantine container should be in the 65° to 70° range, and the container should be isolated from any other aquarium (use separate nets, filters, etc.).

The reason for isolating the new goldfish is to protect your other goldfish from parasites or diseases that it may be harboring. The quarantine container need not be elaborate; a five gallon bucket with a box filter will do for a small to medium sized goldfish. The main point to remember is it must be kept isolated from your other goldfish to prevent accidental contamination of these other goldfish.

I can't state strongly enough about how important quarantining and isolation is. Just take the word of someone (me) who lost 50% of his goldfish through a careless and accidental contamination of his goldfish collection. It happened once and I'll do my best to prevent it happening again.

If at all possible treat sick fish in a quarantine aquarium to prevent destroying the biological balance of your aquarium. Read the manufacturers' directions carefully before doing any treatments.

Parasites (Treat all fish in the infected aquarium)

Fish Lice: A small oval green to brown blood sucking crustacean about the size of a match head (or slightly larger). Treatment: Life Bearer*, Clout*, or Formalite* as directed by the manufacturer. Other petshop products may exist, too.

Anchor Worm: Small slender stick-like crustaceans that are attached to the body, mouth, gills and or fins of a goldfish by a large anchor shaped hook that is imbedded in the tissue of the goldfish. Treatment: Weekly treatments using Clout* or Formalite*, to kill any free swimming young that have recently hatched. Treat the infected fish and aquarium every week for four to six weeks. The adult anchor worm should be gently removed by pulling them out with tweezers. If the anchor worm is attached deeply in the

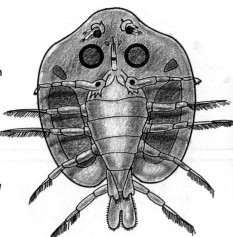

Illustration of Argulus *showing the structures on the ventral side. The large round structures are modified appendages for holding fast to a host fish.*

gills or eye it is better left in place, and a 200 ppm treatment of formalin (37.5% formaldehyde) solution and water should be used as a 60 second dip for five to seven days to kill the anchor worm. If the anchor worm was removed the wound should be treated with an antiseptic.

An anchor worm attached to the skin of a goldfish.

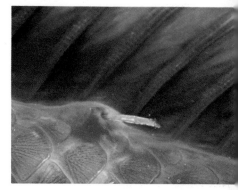

Each spot on the body and fins on this goldfish infected with ich contains numerous spores that upon release develop into ciliated individuals that can infect other fish.

Ich: These small pinhead-sized white spots are a common problem with most fish species. The best cure I've used is Formalite* (although Clout* works well with adult fish), as it can be used on very small goldfish fry effectively at ½ strength. There are many good ich medications on the market that can be used successfully, but be sure to follow the directions carefully.

---

* Formalite is an Aquatronic product. Life Bearer and Clout are products of Aquarium Products.

Velvet: Velvet can be recognized by a patchy dull off-yellow colored area on the fish's body or fins. It is very difficult to detect on an orange goldfish but can be seen as dull areas on a metallic scaled fish. Use one of the commercial products available at your petshop as this is a tough parasite to get rid of.

Costia: This pest is extremely small and in the initial stages of the infection it will cause the goldfish to develop a heavy slime coat, loss of appetite, and will cause the fins to become red and ragged. The only successful treatment I've found is a 25 ppm 37.5% formaldehyde solution (formalin) 24 hour treatment, followed by a 50% water change. The entire aquarium must be treated even though formaldehyde will kill the biological filtration system.

(If possible treat only in quarantine container.)

Bacterial Mouth Fungus or Cottonmouth: This patchy cottony growth is a bacterial infection of the mouth, and is a goldfish killer. Treatment must start early to be effective. Tetracycline is the antibiotic that I would recommend be used, as it's proven to be effective in cases of cottonmouth.

Furunculosis: In the early stages this disease will form small bumps under the scales. These bumps will later enlarge and rupture and form large ulcers on the body of the infected fish. Furunculosis is mainly a cold water disease and is very contagious. All fish in the infected aquarium should be treated in the aquarium even if they show no signs of the disease. The goldfish which shows active signs of the disease should be destroyed or removed to a quarantine container for treatment.

Treatment: Tetracycline bath for 10 days and a medicated food.

Bacterial Fin Rot: There are several antibiotics that can cure this problem and they are readily available at your local petshop. The early signs of this disease are cloudy fins with enlarged blood vessels progressing to split fins and fin erosion. Follow the direction on the antibiotics label and do not rush the treatment. A word of warning: *Costia* and fin congestion have similar symptoms. Antibiotics will not cure these diseases.

Fungus
Fungus can be treated using dyes (methylene blue, malachite green, etc.) applied directly to the fungus if it is localized. Dyes can be used as a dip, or the entire quarantine container can be treated. Some antibiotics are effective against fungus, and your petshop will have a selection from which you can choose. Fungus is generally

Appearance of a sore caused by furunculosis on a rainbow trout. Goldfish are susceptible to furunculosis, and the same type of sore will develop in infected goldfish.

recognized by fuzzy cottony growths on the body or fins.

On headgrowth goldfish breeds (Oranda, Lionhead, Ranchu, etc.) white fungus type growths will often appear. This is usually a sign that the headgrowth is developing and enlarging. At times food may become lodged in the crevices of the headgrowth and will form small balls of fungus. In most cases this type of fungus can be ignored, or you can apply one drop of methylene blue directly to the spot for two to three days or until the fungus is eliminated.

A common goldfish with fungus infection. Note the white areas where the fungal filaments are growing.

Injuries

If the injury is minor like a torn fin or a few missing scales all the hobbyist needs to do (if anything) is add one teaspoon of salt to every five gallons of water in the aquarium. For deep cuts, an antiseptic like mercurochrome, or one of the commercial products available at your petshop, should be applied to the wound. Unfortunately these medications have a hard time sticking to the wound because of the slime coat of a goldfish. But I've found to apply medication to a wound all one needs to do is to take a dry, soft, clean paper towel and pat (do not rub) the wound to slightly dry the area. Quickly apply the medication and release the fish. If the wound is bad, the goldfish should be removed to a quarantine container to recover.

Constipation

The fish affected by this problem will become inactive and will usually have a general swelling of the abdomen. The cause of this problem is usually the rapid eating of large amounts of dry food that absorbs the water in the intestine, causing an intestinal impaction.

If recognized early, this problem can be treated by feeding live or soft foods like *Daphnia*, redworms, duckweed, or homemade soft foods. It would also be helpful to raise the water temperature in a quarantine aquarium to 75° to 80° to encourage the fish to eat these foods, and to increase its metabolism.

Unfortunately the majority of constipation cases are recognized too late, and are often times fatal. It is better to avoid this problem by proper feeding and pre-soaking dried foods.

Fin Congestion

The early signs of this problem are enlarged blood vessels and red spots in the finnage. This problem is usually caused by poor water quality (high ammonia levels, etc.) and in most cases it can be cured by a water change and one to five teaspoons of salt per five gallons of water.

For bad cases place the goldfish in a quarantine container with a good mechanical filter and treat with Tetrocycline to reduce the chances of a bacterial or fungus infection.

There is a scarring problem with fin congestion, and even when cured it will leave enlarged blood vessels and opaque scars in the finnage. Fin congestion is easily prevented by maintaining good water quality, and if you pay special attention to your water quality this environmental disease will never be a problem.

Dropsy

Dropsy is easily recognized by the swelling of the abdomen until the scales stand out from the body of goldfish. This problem is usually fatal unless treatment is started early with a food containing an antibiotic. If the disease is bacterial in nature, and if it hasn't progressed too far, then the goldfish may recover.

Dropsy is at times caused by the effects of high levels of ammonia or nitrate poisoning. If dropsy is caused by these chemical poisons there is no cure, and the goldfish should be

The bloated appearance of this chocolate Oranda is caused by dropsy or excessive accumulation of body fluids in the abdominal cavity.

disposed of humanely.

Goldfish with dropsy should be isolated from other fish to prevent the chance of this disease spreading, if it is contagious. Goldfish with dropsy can live many weeks with this disease, and it would be more humane to dispose of the infected fish after two weeks of treatment, if the fish shows no signs of improvement.

Swimbladder Problems

Fancy goldfish tend to have more of this problem than most other fish. This is probably due to their shortened bodies which misshapes the swimbladder, although disease, constipation and over-feeding can cause this problem. Swim bladder problems in young goldfish usually start to

Disease

Tail rot is one of the diseases a goldfish can contract. Tail rot is the effect of several disease agents, each one treatable by specific medication.

show up when they're three to four months old and are usually genetic in nature. These are not curable.

Another cause of swim bladder problems is food related. If an adult round bodied fancy goldfish swallows air while feeding from the surface, it may end up floating like a cork. This problem is usually self correcting in a day or two, and there is nothing the hobbyist can do to correct it except to change to a food that does not float on the water surface.

Goldfish that are too fat can develop swimbladder problems, as can goldfish which are constipated and those females heavy with eggs. In these cases, if they are treated early, a cure can be brought about by reducing the amount of food you feed, and if possible change to an easily digested or laxative type food like duckweed,

redworm, bloodworm and some moist or semi-moist homemade foods.

Formaldehyde Treatment
This is a very effective cure for many parasite problems, but it is *not* the safest treatment available. The hobbyist must remain near the goldfish that are being treated to watch for the goldfish to show signs of stress, and to take corrective action (water changes) at the first sign of problems. The hobbyist will need to be very careful when handling formaldehyde as the fumes and liquid are very irritating to skin, eyes and lungs.

The hobbyist must treat the entire aquarium in the case of a parasite infection. Formaldehyde will kill plants and will severely disrupt the biological balance of an aquarium, so the hobbyist

Formalin is a toxic compound and should be applied with caution. Follow closely the directions for the proper dose and use of this drug.

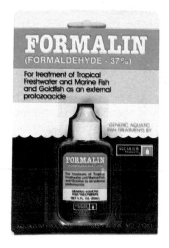

needs to remove all plants and reduce the feeding schedule to prevent poor water quality conditions.

To use this treatment the hobbyist needs to purchase at the local pharmacy, a formalin solution of 37.5% formaldehyde, and a plastic syringe marked in milliliters (or cc's). For every ten gallons of water add one milliliter (or 1 cc) of formalin; this gives an approximate 25 ppm treatment dose of formaldehyde. Formalin is heavier than water so be sure to use adequate circulation in the aquarium.

At the first signs of stress (heavy breathing near the surface), or in eight to twelve hours, change 50% of the water and replace it with fresh treated water of the correct temperature. Repeat this treatment in seven days to treat for any newly hatched parasites.

Warning: If a goldfish is in a very weakened condition, chances are it will not survive this treatment.

Progressive Salt Treatment
When in doubt as to the nature of a disease, or even if there is a disease problem, salt can be added to the aquarium at the rate of one to five teaspoons to every five gallons of water as a tonic to help the fish recover. This low dose treatment generally will not harm plants or the biological balance of an aquarium. The hobbyist should use non-iodized kosher salt or sea salt for any treatment.

The progressive salt treatment should be done in a quarantine

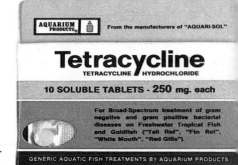

Tetracyline is marketed in both tablet and capsule-enclosed powder form.

aquarium for best results. The progressive salt treatment is generally effective against fungus and some parasite problems. It is a poor treatment for bacterial infections. It can be used in conjunction with heat or not (for goldfish 85° in a very roomy isolation container is considered the top heat range).

The progressive salt treatment takes 10 days to complete.

Nitrofurazone is a well known medication for furunculosis and fungus.

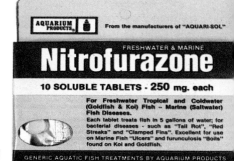

A male goldfish with an unidentified tumor growing behind the operculum. The tumor can be harmless.

(1) Days one through three add one teaspoon of salt for every gallon of water every morning and one teaspoon of salt every night.

(2) Days four through seven, observe goldfish for signs of improvements. If there is no improvement by day seven, continue for another three days.

(3) Days eight through 10, remove 50% of the water each day and replace with fresh aged (or treated) water of the correct temperature.

With the progressive salt treatment use adequate filtration with fresh carbon in the filter.

Medicated Food

For every cup of cooled but not set Gelatin Food (see *Homemade Foods*), add one capsule of tetracycline or other antibiotic. Feed two to three times a day. Feed for at least 10 days, but no more than 14 days.

Humane Disposal of a Terminally Ill Goldfish

Many goldfish diseases do not respond to medication. After a period of two weeks of treatment it would be better to end the suffering of an infected goldfish if it shows no signs of recovery.

The most humane way to end the life of a goldfish is to place it in a container of water and place it in the freezer until it is frozen solid.

Goldfish are coldwater fish and as the water temperature drops, so does their metabolism and awareness. By adding a little salt to the water the goldfish will die very quietly before the water freezes.

After the fish has frozen it should be buried deeply in the flower garden (not vegetable garden) or disposed of in such a way as to comply with city and state regulations.

Spawning Goldfish

If one takes into consideration that in a natural environment goldfish are seasonal spawners, they could be considered a very easy egg layer to spawn. In fact, given just the bare minimum of conditioning, most goldfish will spawn readily. Add to this the fact that the eggs of goldfish are very easy to care for and hatch, and the fry, if given good growing conditions, are very tough and grow very rapidly. It makes goldfish a great egg layer for the novice.

Unfortunately spawning goldfish has one main draw back. The very fancy and rare goldfish breeds do not breed true to type in large numbers, with each spawn only producing a very small number of quality fish (if any). Luckily there are fancy goldfish breeds that do breed reasonably true to type. Fantails, Fringetails, Ryukins, Comets and Pearlscales are a few goldfish breeds that are good for the beginner.

For the patient goldfish breeder who enjoys the challenge of long term line breeding, or who wants the challenge of creating their very own goldfish breed, then the goldfish will offer a lifetime of ever changing genetic challenges.

Breeding is initiated by the male chasing a female that is ready to breed. Note the much enlarged abdomen of this female in comparison to the male on the right.

With their bodies positioned side to side, the female releases her eggs, which are immediately fertilized by the male. This is accompanied by body vibrations and flapping of fins.

Spawning

Remembering that goldfish are seasonal spawners, the hobbyist will find that goldfish are more dependable spawners if they have gone through a period of cold water and reduced food intake hibernation. This is not to say goldfish will not spawn without a hibernation period, it just means they are more dependable spawners with a hibernation period.

A hibernation period of six to eight weeks at a water temperature of 35° to 50° is usually enough to stimulate the spawning urge. Remember that goldfish must be eased slowly into and out of hibernation by slow temperature changes. Feeding during hibernation must be carefully monitored to prevent overfeeding and poor water quality. Feeding is unnecessary in water temperatures below 45°.

For those unable to hibernate the goldfish in cold water, the hobbyist should reduce the amount of food available to the spawners for a four to six week period. This allows the goldfish to use up its fat reserves, which is important as a fat goldfish is usually not eager to spawn and a fat female is prone to egg binding.

After the hibernation period, the diet of the goldfish should include such high protein foods as redworm, bloodworm, scrambled egg, and high protein prepared foods. This rich diet encourages healthy egg and sperm production. With proper

Note the breeding tubercles on the surface of the operculum of this male Chinese Lionhead.

An inexpensive digital thermometer will be adequate for determining the approximate temperature of the aquarium water. A very precise and expensive thermometer is not necessary.

food, lots of room and good water quality your goldfish will usually be in spawning condition in six to ten weeks after coming out of their hibernating period.

If you have a large number of goldfish to select your spawners from, you should select only those goldfish that have the desired breed characteristics, and those that compliment and balance each other. This selection takes a great deal of study and the hobbyists must know their breed and its standards very well in order to mate their goldfish to best advantage.

Under no circumstances should the inexperienced or casual goldfish hobbyist spawn goldfish that are not all of the same breed. This type of mixed breed cross will only produce garbage in the majority of cases, as many goldfish breed characteristics are genetically recessive. Mixed breed crosses should only be attempted by the hobbyist who can devote the time and aquarium space to carry these crosses through four to five generations.

Goldfish are not easy fish to sex when they are not in spawning condition.

During the spawning season the females will have a swelling in the abdomen region; some tend to be fuller in one side than the other. The male goldfish will develop breeding tubercles during the spawning season. These small white bumps are located on the gill covers and the leading rays of the pectoral fin.

When not in spawning condition the male goldfish usually has longer pectoral fins than the female of the same breed, and the leading rays of the pectoral fins will be larger (thicker) than the female's. Females are usually larger than the males, and will have a broader body when viewed from above.

Sexing goldfish is difficult even for the experienced hobbyist. If possible, when buying breeding stock, try to buy five to seven fish so your odds of getting a pair will be increased.

In a natural environment goldfish are school spawners, and the males in any spawning group should out–number the females. Many goldfish hobbyists prefer the pair (one male, one female) and the trio (two males, one female) methods of mating their goldfish. These

This photo illustrates the great variability of a character like the red cap in these Lionheads. A discriminating goldfish hobbyist will reject those with imperfect caps.

two methods allow spawning aquariums of 20 to 50 gallons to be used for spawning. The size of the spawning aquarium is determined by the size of the spawners and their total numbers. Goldfish that are crowded into a too small aquarium will not spawn readily, so care must be taken to give them plenty of room.

The spawning aquariums should be of the long and low types, as this gives the spawners room for the usually very active spawning chase. Also these types of aquariums are preferred as the aquarium should only have a water depth of six to ten inches, as goldfish prefer to spawn in shallow water.

Goldfish have a wide spawning temperature range and may start to spawn as their water reaches 60°, but for the proper development of the eggs and the resulting fry the water temperature should be 68°.

The subject of the correct temperature to incubate goldfish eggs has never been and probably never will be settled. From my own experiences I am inclined to believe that for proper tail fin development in the double tailed breeds a temperature of 68° is the best temperature to achieve fully split double tail fins. Any warmer and a lot of web and tripod tail fish develop; any colder and the fry tend to be weak and lack vigor.

Since many goldfish breeds have been developed in tropical countries, many of these fish have never seen a water temperature below 70°, and yet

Goldfish eggs in different stages of development. The fully hatched fry at the bottom of the picture is ready to swim, while the one on the left is still partly within the egg membrane.

they have beautifully split tail fins. I'm not really all that sure that the fully split double tail fin is heavily dependent on water temperature since I'm sure genetics play a very major role in the development of any goldfish breed characteristic. I'll stick with 68° as the ideal spawning and incubation temperature, as I've had better results at that temperature than any other temperature.

Goldfish spawn adhesive eggs, and in nature these eggs adhere to underwater plants and the roots of floating plants. Those eggs that settle in the mud at the bottom of a lake or pond usually do not develop. In the aquarium the hobbyist should provide spawning material for the eggs to adhere to and to help stimulate the goldfish into spawning.

The lively activity of spawning is captured in this photo. The spawning partners move throughout the tank, even breaking through the water surface.

A goldfish spawning mop can easily be made by wrapping nylon yarn around a six inch book fifty times. Cut the yarn from the book in one place and then tie the strand in the middle to form a loose mop. This mop can be floated by attaching it to a cork, or by using an empty 35mm plastic film canister, or it can be used with no float as bottom spawning material.

For best results floating and bottom spawning material should be used in the spawning aquarium. The spawning material should be isolated in one end of

the aquarium to encourage the goldfish to spawn in that area, this will make it easier to remove the eggs to a hatchery aquarium if you want to.

Many fine leafed aquarium plants can be used for goldfish to spawn on, and plants like Water Hyacinth and Water Lettuce have long dense roots that make good spawning sites. Make sure when using natural plants that they are free of harmful pests, such as snails, hydra, etc.

For those who don't have the time to make their own spawning material, or who lack natural plants for spawning material, there is always your local petshop. Your local petshop has, or can get readymade artificial spawning material for several different types that are great to use with egg layers.

Many hobbyists will set up the spawning aquarium (the spawning material should be added later to keep it clean) and then place the female(s) in it for the pre-spawning conditioning period. As the female reaches spawning condition, she will start to swell noticeably in the abdomen as her eggs enlarge and develop. The male(s) will usually develop breeding tubercules as they get into spawning condition.

When the hobbyist feels that the goldfish are ready to spawn, the male(s) are placed in the spawning aquarium with the female(s) and the spawning material set in place. If all the goldfish are in spawning condition there should be eggs by the hundreds, or more than likely thousands, in the spawning aquarium in two or three days. Many times this doesn't happen, and the spawners can be separated or left together for an additional conditioning period.

When goldfish are through spawning, they should be removed quickly from the spawning aquarium, or the eggs should be promptly removed to a hatchery aquarium. Goldfish once through spawning will eat the eggs a lot faster than they spawned them. Masses of dense spawning material and prompt

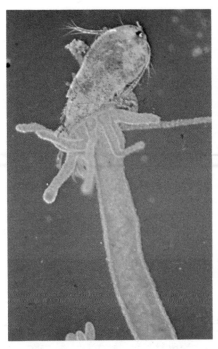

Hydras are free-living animals which can pose a threat to fry in a breeding tank. The hydra shown here is devouring a crustacean, but the victim could just as easily have been a goldfish.

removal of spawners or eggs after the spawners are through spawning will keep egg losses to a minimum. Also keep an eye open for any goldfish not taking an active part in the spawn, as they will spend their time eating eggs as fast as they find them.

Goldfish are morning spawners, and will start spawning at dawn and finish in two to four hours. When you set up your spawners you should keep this in mind and try to plan the spawn when you will be available to watch over the spawn and save the eggs.

This seine photographed on a commercial goldfish hatchery in the United States is reported to contain as many as 85,000 Fantails. Of course one can not expect the same succes in the breeding of the very fancy breeds.

Dead eggs appear opaque and those already attacked by fungus have a layer of fungal filaments.

From time to time you will have males that are unwilling to start spawning even though the female is more than ready. This bit of bad luck usually happens when breeding in pairs. Often these reluctant males can get into the spawning mood by the introduction of another male goldfish who is in spawning condition. Once the spawning chase has started and eggs are laid this odd male should be removed, and the more desirable male will usually continue to spawn. For this method a male of any goldfish breed can be used, as the few eggs he may fertilize will only be a small part of the total spawn if he is removed early.

Raising the Fry
After the eggs have been laid the hobbyist can either remove the eggs to another aquarium, or remove the adult spawners and allow the eggs to hatch where they were laid.

When moving the eggs it is impossible to remove them all, as many are attached to the aquarium. The few eggs left behind are usually no great loss, as the average goldfish spawn of 500 to 3,000 eggs is many more than the average hobbyist can cope with. Remember goldfish fry *cannot* be crowded, so don't worry about a few lost eggs as you'll be kept busy with the ones you save on the spawning material.

Fertile goldfish eggs are usually resistant to fungus attacks if they are kept in water that has a low organic content and good water quality. Not all goldfish eggs in a spawn get fertilized. The hobbyist who gets a consistent 75% fertility rate in a natural spawn can consider this a very good average. Now a 75% fertility rate when compared to the spawn of some other egg layers is not really all that great, but once again you need to consider that just the average sized two year old female is going to spawn 1,500 to 3,000 eggs every ten to fourteen days during the spawning season. This kind of egg production makes it difficult for the average hobbyist to raise just one spawn, let alone every spawn.

At 68° the infertile eggs will turn an opaque milky white in about 24 hours. The almost clear fertile eggs will take about four days to hatch at 68°, and the fry will become free swimming and start to search for food in about two days after hatching. The unfertilized eggs usually fungus.

While the eggs are developing

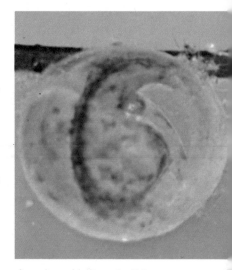

An enlarged image of a living goldfish embryo. The embryo is protected by the surrounding embryonic fluid and a tough egg membrane outside.

A closeup of a newly hatched goldfish fry. The eyes are relatively large and the yolk sac is fairly large at this stage.

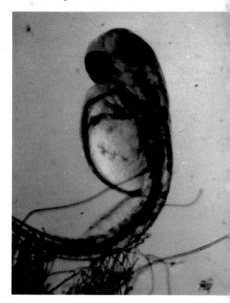

Shown is a fully hatched brine shrimp nauplius and another one that has just hatched out of its chitinous egg shell.

they need a steady gentle stream of circulating water to insure they receive enough oxygen to develop properly. This gentle water movement can easily be provided by a slow stream of bubbles from an airstone, sponge filter or portable undergravel filter. This gentle stream of air also should keep any surface scum from developing. This is important for a free exchange of gases at the water's surface.

When the fry become free swimming slowly raise the water temperature to 74°. This increases their metabolism and food consumption which has the desirable effect of increasing their growth rate.

Just as soon as the fry become free swimming the hobbyist will have to furnish the fry with *proper food* and *good water quality* to insure rapid growth. To make it easy to refer to each item, they will be covered separately.

Feeding the Fry: The trick to feeding goldfish fry is to provide enough food of the right size for rapid growth, and to do so without overfeeding and polluting their water.

Newly hatched goldfish fry are fairly large for the fry of an egglayer, so very small foods like infusoria or green water are usually not necessary. When the fry become free swimming a good first food can be made from a hard boiled egg yolk liquified in a blender. This liquified hard boiled egg yolk can be fed to the fry at the rate of one to three drops per gallon (depending on the number of fry in the aquarium), two or three times a day. Be very careful with egg yolk as it is very high in protein, decomposes quickly, and is considered a *very highly polluting food*. A few small Ramshorn or other small mouthed snails can help to clean up some excess food, but don't rely on them too heavily.

Liquified hard boiled egg yolk only needs to be fed for the first four to five days, as the fry grow very quickly eating it and will need a larger food. Newly hatched baby brine shrimp is the next food easily available to many hobbyists, and it is a very good food for raising small goldfish fry. You should start feeding a small amount of baby brine shrimp starting on the third feeding day, and slowly phase out the egg yolk while increasing the baby brine shrimp.

A word to the wise: Never make any food change too quickly! Always overlap the food changes to allow the fry a chance to recognize the new food and adapt to it.

Baby brine shrimp is a very good food for goldfish fry for the first three weeks, at which time other foods can, and should be introduced. Fry foods like microworms, screened baby *Daphnia* and finely powdered dry food are all good. As the fry get larger, soft paste foods and gelatin foods can be introduced, as soon as they are large enough to eat them.

To successfully feed and raise goldfish fry, the hobbyist needs to carefully watch the fry to make sure they are eating enough without alot of waste which will pollute the water. To keep overfeeding problems to a minimum, feed a small amount of food often. Use snails and a good filtration system to help maintain good water quality.

Water Quality in the Fry Aquarium: To maintain good water quality in the fry aquarium four items need to be carefully attended to, these are: filtration, frequent syphoning of solid wastes, frequent small water changes, and an uncrowded aquarium by frequent and heavy culling.

Filtration: Preferably this should be of the biological type, and can be furnished by using the commercial sponge filter, a small version of the portable tray filter, or a box filter filled with coarse gravel or bone charcoal and then wrapped with quilt batting to keep the fry from being sucked into the filter. All of these filters should be of the air operated types, at least at first as power filters create too much of a water current.

Many hobbyists who raise goldfish fry prefer to raise their fry in an aquarium with no gravel on the aquarium bottom. A bare aquarium is easier to clean, but the main advantage of a bare

Ramshorn snails (genus Planorbis) *are among the types generally available at pet shops.*

slow syphon, which, with luck, and a little practice, doesn't suck too many goldfish out of the aquarium as you are removing the solid wastes. The few fry who are sucked out of the aquarium can be quickly recaptured, especially if you have syphoned them into a large white bowl which makes them easy to see.

A small daily partial water change is a very big benefit in raising goldfish fry. It encourages rapid growth and good health, and is well worth the time needed to complete. To quickly syphon out a small amount of water from the fry aquarium, wrap the end of the syphon hose with quilt batting, filter floss, or insert it into a sponge. This allows you to quickly syphon out enough water for a water change, without the fear or hassle of getting a bucket (or bowl) full of goldfish fry; or use an automatic water changer.

The amount of water that you change really depends on the number of fry in the aquarium. Given an uncrowded aquarium with a good filtration system, a 5% to 10% daily water change is all that is needed.

In adding water to the fry aquarium, try to keep the water level at about six to eight inches for the first two weeks. The water level can then *slowly* be increased over the next four weeks to 10–16 inches.

Culling: To successfully raise goldfish fry they *cannot* be crowded! A 20 gallon long aquarium can hold approximately 500 fry until they

This English biological filter is an excellent filter to maintain good water quality in this goldfish fry aquarium.

aquarium is that very little food is lost, as the fry can find any food that has settled to the bottom.

The fry aquarium needs to have any solid fry and snail wastes and uneaten food removed frequently to keep them from polluting the water. A handy tool for this job is a length of air line tubing with a 12 inch piece of rigid, clear plastic tubing attached to one end. This is a are 10 days old. At 10 days of age the fry need to be culled down to 100 fry for every 144 square inches of surface area (12" × 12"). Using frequent cullings, at the age of four weeks the fry should be culled down to 30 fry for every 144 square inches of surface area. By the time the fry are eight weeks old they should be maintained at the same density as an adult goldfish (30 square inches to every inch of goldfish body).

It's difficult for the beginning goldfish breeder to part with any of his baby goldfish. But since fancy goldfish only breed true to type in very small numbers, if the hobbyist doesn't cull heavily then the hobbyist is going to raise a lot of substandard goldfish, have many health problems due to overcrowding, have slow growth rates, and spend a lot of money needlessly on fry foods.

When the fry hatch they are not much more than two eyes connected to a slender tail. By the time they are ten days old they are large enough to cull for some basic features.

The first item to cull for are the eyes. Make sure they have two of them! The body shape and size is the next item. Crooked bodies and bent spines are fairly easy to cull for. Runts (those smaller than average) should all be culled, as they will seldom develop into anything worth keeping. Those fry having difficulty in swimming properly should all be culled.

The last item to cull for at ten days of age is the tail fin. In every spawning of fancy double tailed goldfish you will have some fry with a single tail fin. By culling from above, these single tail fry are easily separated from their double tail tank mates.

Small goldfish fry are easily damaged when handled during cullings. When the fry are small, a large kitchen baster is a handy culling tool. For larger fry a very fine small net (brine shrimp net) will help prevent any damage. When moving goldfish fry with a net, only move a few at a time, or better still use a small bowl or cup to catch or move goldfish

Automatic water changers are helpful in maintaining the quality of the water in an aquarium.

This young five-month-old Oranda has just completed its color change and should be totally orange in about a week or two.

fry. In fact a good rule of thumb while culling is only to net those fish that are to be culled. All others are moved by using a bowl or cup.

As the fry develop, many defects can be spotted like long bodies, straight backs, bent fins, poor swimming ability, small size, webtail fins, tripod tails, poor finnage size, unequal fin development, and late coloring, just to mention a few. These items should be watched for and the defective fry culled regularly.

Metallic goldfish fry are basically an olive green color until they start to change colors. Nacreous fry are a grayish to pinkish color initially, and matt fry start out their lives as a pale pink color with solid black eyes.

The time it takes for a goldfish fry to start to change to its adult color will vary from as little as 60 days, to as long as three years,

and in some cases a few fry in each spawn will never change colors at all.

Orange, red and white metallic goldfish will go through a darkening phase before they change to their adult color. These fry will slowly change from their immature olive green color to almost black, then they will quickly start to lose this black pigment on the abdomen and the adult color will fade out the rest of the black usually in a short time. After the young metallic goldfish has changed color, it is often very pale when compared with the adult color. Luckily the color will darken as time goes by, especially if the fry are exposed to natural sunlight for a few hours each day.

Black, bluescale, brown and calico goldfish do not go through a dark phase before coloring. These colors will slowly appear on the young goldfish and will build intensity as the fish age. Calicos color up very early, but it may take as long as two years before the colors stabilize and become fixed. Calicos are difficult to breed for color because of this changing color behavior, but the development of a good calico strain is well worth the effort.

Culling for breed characteristics (i.e. headgrowth, finnage, bubble eyes, eye growth, nasal growth, etc.) will take many months or years, as many of these characteristics may take years to develop, and are affected by careful feeding, good water quality and lots of care.

Basic Fancy Goldfish Breeds

When the subject of goldfish is brought up, the novice will immediately visualize the common goldfish in a small glass bowl. But to the knowledgeable goldfish hobbyist the word "goldfish" brings to mind dozens of different basic breeds with many variations possible within each breed.

The word "goldfish" is a general term used in describing the group. It's much like saying "dog, horse or chicken" to describe a group of domestic animals that man has, over the centuries, molded through careful selective breeding into an animal that bears little or no resemblance to its originating ancestor.

This section is not meant to be a specific standard for each breed described. Its main purpose is to help the novice and others interested in goldfish, in the identification, selection and in some cases cultural requirements of some of the more common breeds of fancy goldfish.

The novice and more experienced hobbyist should be aware that some goldfish breeds which are raised in different countries of the world will vary considerably from each other. Orandas probably exhibit the greatest change from country to country, and the Red Cap Oranda seems to exhibit the greatest differences within the same breed. Due to its popularity, many countries have been breeding the Redcap with dozens of different body shapes, head growths, finnage styles, and yet they all have the same

A white Oranda with fantail and red cap.

basic color pattern for which this breed is known.

So given these geographical variations, I will do my best in this section to give general descriptions in hopes of helping you with the selection of some of the popular imported and domestic fancy goldfish. It is my hope that the goldfish hobbyist will use this section as intended, as a general guide.

This section is not meant as a goldfish standard, and in fact the American Goldfish Standards published by the Goldfish Society of America may differ greatly from the goldfish breeds that are being imported into our country. The reason for this is simple, the American goldfish breeders have their own opinion of what a breed of goldfish should look like. Other countries have their own standards, but all strive for basically the same goals.

Although this variation within a single goldfish breed may lead to some confusion, it gives goldfish hobbyists a wonderful selection to choose from and enjoy. After all isn't *variety* the spice of life?

Single Tail Goldfish Breeds

Comet: I can only think of a very few people who have had the pleasure of seeing a really high quality Comet. This American goldfish breed has a very long, deeply forked single tail fin at least twice (or more) as long as the long slim body. The dorsal fin, and all other fins are extremely long, making this breed a graceful and showy goldfish.

Although hundreds of millions of Comet and Comet-like goldfish are sold every year, good quality Comets are as hard

The high dorsal fin and long pointed tail indicate that this young Comet (five months old) has the potential of developing into a first class fish.

A Bristol Shubunkin. No two of this breed will have the same color pattern.

to find as many of the rare double tail goldfish breeds.

The basic color of a Comet should be bright deep red orange (almost red), and red and white.

The Comet is really at its best as a pond fish. It is very hardy and survives winter hibernation under ice if the pond is deep enough to prevent it from freezing solid.

Shubunkins: In Great Britain there are two basic single tail Shubunkin breeds. The short finned London, and the long tail finned broad lobed Bristol Shubunkin.

We Americans have two basic types of these single tail breeds. These are the short finned Common Shubunkin and the long finned American (Comet-type) Shubunkin.

In selecting a Shubunkin for color, look for bright reds, jet black, pure white and large patches of sky blue. Since no two Shubunkins are colored alike, the hobbyists can pick the color pattern that is most attractive to them. This variable color pattern is what makes the Shubunkin (and other Calico breeds) so popular.

The Shubunkin has a long slender body and does very well in a pond environment.

Double Tail Fancy Goldfish
Double tail goldfish breeds have two things in common, that is they have two tail fins and two anal fins.

The two side-by-side tail fins should be completely separated from each other, although it is acceptable to have the tail fin partially joined if it has no more than 10% joined along the top edge. Each tail fin should have two well formed lobes of equal size and shape, giving the double tail breeds four tail fin lobes.

The only exceptions to this rule are the Tosakin, which has the tails joined at the top, and the Lionhead, Ranchu, and Chinese Pom Pom where partially webbed tail fins are acceptable at the present time.

There are many variations in the double tail fins. Some are very long (Fringetails), some when viewed from above will look like butterfly wings (Butterfly Tails), some have broad tail fin lobes while others have very thin and long lobes (Ribbon Tails), then there are those few breeds that have no indentation between the tail fin lobes (Veils) while others will have very deep forks. Some breeds have short, medium or long fins and if this wasn't confusing enough, the

angle at which the tail fin is held in relation to the caudal peduncle is a very important feature of many of the double tail breeds.

It is impossible to describe every type of tail fin found in double tail goldfish breeds. I'll try to simplify definitions by using simple terms like "long" or "short" to describe the tail fin of a goldfish breed. But one of the most important features the goldfish hobbyist must look for when selecting double tail fin goldfish is the ability of the fish to carry and swim with this finnage. If a goldfish lacks the proper body shape, swim bladder function and strength to carry and swim smoothly with their finnage, they are of little use to the hobbyist, as these

A Fringetail bred in Japan.

The red and white pattern in this Ryukin is eye-catching.

goldfish lack the swimming grace for which the double tail breeds are known.

Fantail: When compared to the single tail breeds, this double tail breed has a short round body, but for the double tail breeds this goldfish breed has one of the longer bodies of the double tail breeds.

The Fantail has medium length fins with the tail fin about ½ to ¾ as long as the body. This is a very hardy breed, and it is one of the best double tail breeds for the novice. Fantails are a good pond fish, being hardy and very active. Fantails come in most goldfish colors.

Fringetails: This beautiful goldfish breed has a fairly long body by double tail goldfish standards. The very long double tail fins should be 1½ to 2 times as long as the body (or longer).

The Fringetail is another goldfish breed that is a good goldfish for those who want to gain experience with keeping fancy goldfish, as they are reasonably priced and are hardy enough for the pond.

Fringetails can be found in most goldfish colors.

Ryukin: The Ryukin has a very round body and exhibits what is commonly called a humped back. This highly arched back adds to the roundness of the body and can be easily selected for in young Ryukins.

The finnage should be at least as long as the body to 1½ times the body length or longer, if the fish has the strength to handle these extra long tail fins. The lobes of the tail fin should be fairly wide with a definite deep indentation between the lobes.

The calico coloration of this young calico Ryukin is nearly perfect. If the body and finnage all grow properly this young goldfish will be of show quality.

The color of the Ryukin is usually orange, which in the better fish is almost red. Red and white, brown, white, and calico are all colors available in the Ryukin breed, and all colors should be bright and well defined. The Calico Ryukin's body is not nearly as round as the red and white, and red Ryukins, which shows that it is a fairly recently developed version of this very old goldfish breed.

Ryukins need a food high in carbohydrates to help in the development of the round full bodies that characterize this breed. Ryukins are a fairly hardy fish, and are well adapted for the ornamental pond if predators are not a problem.

Veiltail: This rare, beautiful American goldfish breed was developed in the Philadelphia region in the late 1920's. The double tail fins are very long (1½ to 2½ times the body length), and in high quality Veiltails, they should have absolutely no forking between the top and bottom tail fin lobes.

The square cut tail fins and the very high dorsal fin (as high as the body is deep) of the Veiltail is usually found on a round bodied fish with a pointed head and no headgrowth.

Even though Veiltails are a difficult goldfish breed to spawn and raise high quality individuals from, the veil characteristic is fairly easy to breed into other goldfish breeds, only taking two generations to do so initially, and a mere 10 to 20 years of strict line breeding to perfect (hopefully). But that's the only easy part in Veiltail breeding, which probably explains why they are so rare, with only a handful of American hobbyists breeding them.

Veiltails in America can be found being bred in calico, orange, red and white, and black (Moors) colors. The Veiltail characteristic has also been bred into the Telescope (Moor) and Oranda breeds, but only in a limited number by a very few American goldfish breeders.

Photographed from this position, the superb and delicate finnage of this red cap Oranda is displayed at its best.

This is the result of a cross between a Ryukin and a Veiltail. Both parental features are present in this specimen.

Pearlscales: The Pearlscale has often been described as a baseball with warts. In fact, a four-year-old well cared for adult will have the body shape and size of a baseball with fins.

This unique breed gets its name from its very own scale type. In the center of each scale is a raised bump, which is usually white in color, and if you use your imagination it can appear to look like a half pearl has been glued to each scale. These unique scales show up very early on a young Pearlscale, and in better specimens they will get larger and more pronounced as the Pearlscale ages. A good quality Pearlscale will have every scale pearled, including those on the back, which on poorer specimens have little or no pearling.

The body of a Pearlscale is probably the roundest and shortest of any goldfish breed. The measurement taken from the base of the dorsal to the bottom of the belly will nearly equal the measurement taken from the base of the head to the base of the tail fin.

Pearlscales can be bred into any goldfish color and scale type (metallic, nacreous, and matt). But because of the opaque raised center of each scale metallic goldfish can look a lot like nacreous scaled goldfish, because if the pearl center is very large it will cover the reflective quanine layer. The most common colors seen in Pearlscales are orange, red and white, white and calico. The other colors are rare, but do show up from time to time in

The characteristic bump on each scale is evident on all the scales of this Pearl-scale.

Basic Fancy Goldfish Breeds

shipments of imported goldfish.

This double tail breed was thought to be one of the originating breeds that helped to develop the American Veiltail, because one of its breed characteristics is a square forkless tail fin. Although the modern Pearlscale can now be found with short Veiltail-like tail fins, long Veiltail-like tail fins and long forked tail fins.

The diet of a Pearlscale should be closely monitored to prevent the fish from becoming overweight. This breed suffers from swimbladder problems slightly more than other breeds and over-eating can cause the swim bladder to malfunction.

Orandas: Oranda is a general term used to describe a breed of double tail, short, round bodied goldfish with a bumpy type of headgrowth. This headgrowth can include all areas of the head (top, cheeks and gill covers), or be limited to just one area of the head (usually the top of the head). This headgrowth can be modest or it can be huge like that found in high quality Lionheads. Good Orandas are rare, as only a small percentage of a spawn of Orandas will develop a proper headgrowth. Then if you take into consideration finnage, body shape, color and all the defects these items can have, you can see why a good quality Oranda is a hard fish to find.

The body style of Orandas will vary from oval, to egg shape, to almost round. Usually you will find that the bigger the tail fin,

the longer the body of an Oranda will be. This extra body length allows for more strength to carry and swim with these very long tail fins. The very short compressed bodies of some Orandas dictate that they have shorter tail fins, but in these fish the tail fin should be at least as long as the body. In the longer tail fin varieties, the tail fin can be as long as two times the body length, although such long finnage is very rare in an Oranda. All Orandas have dorsal fins which should be held high and erect.

Orandas are found in every color and scale group that the goldfish exhibit. Many Orandas are a single color, although some breeds will have two or more colors. In selecting Orandas for color, look for fish with sharp bright well defined colors especially on the belly and the headgrowth.

For an Oranda to develop the headgrowth for which it is known, it must be fed a diet higher in protein than that fed to most non-head growth goldfish breeds. Don't make the food too high in protein though, as the Oranda still needs a fair amount of carbohydrates so that it will develop the round full body that adds to the beauty of this breed.

Dorsal-less Goldfish Breeds

The main distinguishing characteristic of these breeds is the complete lack of a dorsal fin. All other fins are complete, with the double tail fin and double anal fins similar to other double tail goldfish breeds.

The lack of a dorsal fin is not a stable genetic feature (What feature is with goldfish?). Although some line bred dorsal-less breeds that are very well fixed may only have a modest number of offspring in each spawn that will have partial dorsal fins, the opposite is usually the case. The outline along the back of a dorsal-less breed should be a smooth gentle curve from base of head to base of tail fin. There should be no bumps, hollows, dorsal spikes or any other defect along the back. The back should be broad and evenly scaled.

Chinese Lionhead:

The Lionhead is the granddaddy of the dorsal-less headgrowth goldfish breeds. This Chinese breed is often confused with the Japanese Ranchu by the novice, but given high quality adult Lionheads and high quality Ranchus in the same aquarium, even the most inexperienced beginner can tell that they are two different breeds.

The body of the Lionhead is somewhat more boxy and a little longer than the Ranchu. The curve along the back is not as arched in the Lionhead as it is in the Ranchu, and this gentle curve is carried right to the base of the tail. The curve along the back should have no bumps, hollows, or any sign of a dorsal fin.

The finnage of the Chinese Lionhead is very short, being ⅜ to ½ as long as the body. This is one of the few double tailed

Head-on view of a Chinese Lionhead.

Side view of a Chinese Lionhead. Note the shallow arch of the back.

goldfish breeds that can have a partially webbed tail fin (joined along the top edge). Many Lionheads will have butterfly tail fins, and, when viewed, from above this type of tail fin is very attractive.

The biggest difference between the Lionhead and the Ranchu is the headgrowth. In the better adult Lionheads the mass and size of the headgrowth will approach the mass and size of the body, where even in the best Ranchu they will not have a headgrowth that could compare to the huge head mass of the Lionhead. This huge headgrowth covers the entire head and is an unforgettable sight.

The color of the Lionhead comes in orange, red and white, white, calico, and black. Since the Asian breeders have concentrated on headgrowth, the orange color of the Lionhead is generally not as deep in color as that of the Ranchu, but this is not always the case and brightly colored near red Lionheads will turn up from time to time.

The Lionhead, like the Oranda, should be fed a diet high in protein to encourage the development of the headgrowth.

A Japanese Ranchu. Note the relatively short tail fin.

Ranchu: The Japanese Ranchu is the most common and popular of all the dorsal-less breeds. The Ranchu has a short round heavy body. The head is very broad in the better specimens to allow for a full headgrowth. The headgrowth should cover the entire head and be well developed in all areas.

The finnage of the Ranchu is short, with the tail fin about $3/8$ to $1/2$ as long as the body. The double tail fins can be partially joined (webbed) or completely separated. The tail fins are held high and erect, and because of the sudden downward angle change of the backbone near the tail fin, it appears to be attached to the caudal peduncle at a sharp angle.

The Ranchu is sold incorrectly as a Lionhead in most petshops.

The Lionhead is a Chinese breed while the Ranchu is a Japanese breed, and the fact that they both lack dorsal fins and have headgrowths is the only things they have in common.

When these two breeds are very young the easiest way to tell them apart is by body shape. The Ranchu has a definite highly arched curve along the back in the better specimens, with a sharp downward angle change as it nears the caudal peduncle. The Ranchu body shape is more egg shaped when the fish are young, while the Lionhead is more rectangular. The adults of both breeds are easy to tell apart, even by the beginner, who once seeing a mature adult of each breed will realize that there are two breeds of dorsal-less goldfish with a headgrowth.

A black Lionhead, male, one year old. Black Lionheads are very rare and are almost never seen in the average pet shop.

The common color of the Ranchu is orange, red and white, and white. Calico Ranchus have been developed, but they are very rare, so are seldom seen.

The Ranchu should be fed a diet high in protein to encourage a good headgrowth. Since the Ranchu is a large fish with some older adults reaching eight to ten inches in length, they should be given plenty of room in their aquariums.

Ranchus are available in a variety of color patterns.

A pair of Orandas with pom poms. Perfect pom poms are hard to find.

Pom Pom: This Chinese breed has a dorsal-less Lionhead type body with short fins very much like the Lionhead. This breed has a round pea sized growth over each nostril that is formed from the excessive ruffled growth of the nasal septum. This breed is usually seen as a calico (nacreous), but orange and matts are seen from time to time.

When selecting Pom Poms look for smooth backs, bright colors and nasal growths that are of the same size and well colored. Good quality specimens are very rare, so be prepared to accept some defects when buying this breed.

Pom Poms have been bred onto many Orandas but in the dorsal-less Chinese Pom Pom no headgrowth should be seen.

Celestial: To the novice, this breed will appear at first to be a telescope (globe eye), but upon closer examination it will be seen that the pupil of the eyes are looking heavenward. The eyes of a Celestial should be large and of equal size. The pupils should be the same size and be looking straight up or slightly cross eyes. The pupils in this breed vary from very large to pin points, so examine them carefully to make sure they are the same size.

The Celestial's body is long and narrow. The tail fins are fairly long (3/4 to 1 1/4 times body length), which adds beauty and swimming grace to this strange looking breed.

The color is usually orange, red and white, and white.

The Celestial goldfish should be kept in an aquarium or small pond with its own kind, or other eyed goldfish breeds (Telescopes, Bubble Eyes, etc.). A floating food is a benefit to this breed, but it is quite adept at finding food on the bottom. Remove all sharp items from their environment to avoid the fish from damaging themselves.

A dramatic photo depicting the desirable location of the eyes in a Celestial. It is obvious that Celestials are best fed with floating type of food.

A calico Bubble Eye is one color variety of Bubble Eye you are not likely to see very often.

Bubble Eyes: The Bubble Eye is a funny looking fellow, with large bobbing watery bubbles below each eye. With this breed of goldfish you either like it or you don't, there are very few middle of the roaders when it comes to Bubble Eyes. The Bubble Eye is a fairly common breed, but as with many other goldfish breeds, good quality fish are hard to find.

The body of the Bubble Eye comes in two shapes. The first type has a short round Lionhead type body. This type has short fins which are slightly longer than those found in the Lionhead, and they are held higher and more erect.

The second body type is longer and slimmer with a fairly straight back. The finnage is long and flowing (³/₄ to 1¹/₂ times body length), and is held high and well spread. This second body type seems to be the dominant form being imported today. They are very impressive.

The main color of imported Bubble Eyes are orange, red and white, and white. Calico, brown, black and blue scales have been seen, but they are very rare.

The bubbles under each eye can vary in size from small to huge. In some cases the bubbles are wider than the fish is long. But more important than bubble size is how well the fish can carry and swim with these large bubbles. Some Bubble Eyes swim very well with large bubbles and can remain buoyant in any level of the aquarium, while others sink right to the bottom because of the extra weight of the bubbles. When selecting a Bubble Eye pay careful attention to its swimming ability.

The bubbles of a Bubble Eye should attach to the eye as low as possible. In no case should the bubble completely surround the eye and isolate it from the fish's head. The area of attachment should be at the bottom half of the eye as this allows the fish some side vision.

The eyes of some Bubble Eyes may be lifted upward by the bubbles, while on other fish the eyes will remain in the normal position. As long as both eyes are in the same position, either the upward looking or normal eye-position is acceptable.

The Bubble Eye is a dorsal-less breed and should have a smooth back with no signs of a dorsal fin, bumps or hollows.

Bubble Eyes should be kept with their own kind or other eyed types (Telescopes, Celestials, etc.). All sharp objects that can rupture the fragile bubbles should be absent from their aquarium or pond.

A dramatic head-on view of a black Bubble Eye, a rare color in Bubble Eyes.

A Moor of show quality should not have any metallic sheen and must be velvety black.

Telescopes or Globe Eyes: The Globe Eye has been around for centuries and has helped to create many goldfish breeds, lending finnage, bodyshape, and above all color to these breeds.

Whether you call this breed of goldfish a Telescope, which does not describe it correctly, or a Globe Eye makes little difference. What does matter is that the hobbyist is able to select and care for the Globe Eyes properly.

The Globe Eye goldfish exhibit large bulging eyes that gives this fish the appearance of a country boy who has just seen his first X-rated movie. These protruding eyes start to develop very early in the fry's life, usually when the fry is between 60 to 90 days of age. Since the eyes will continue to grow at a slightly faster rate than the body of the Globe Eye for the first year or two, it is hard to judge the eye quality of a Globe Eye until the fish is two years old.

The Globe Eye is one of the more difficult goldfish breeds to find and from which to select good quality fish. There are several different eye shapes found in Globe Eyes and the hobbyist should examine the eyes carefully to make sure that both eyes are the same size and shape. To judge the eye characteristics the hobbyist must not only view the fish from the side, but must view the fish from above to make sure that the eyes protrude from the head at the same angle.

The eyes of the Globe Eye should be as large as possible, and that can be very large in highly developed Globe Eyes. A special item to watch for in selecting Globe Eyes is clouding of the cornea, or the clear covering over the pupil. This clouding can cause blindness as the fish ages, so any clouding should be enough reason to reject the fish.

The body of a high quality Globe Eye is short, round and egg shaped. Since this is a goldfish breed that is popular and always in demand, the large domestic hatcheries are producing this breed by the millions each year. The domestic Globe Eyes tend to be much too long in body, and can grow to ten inches in length if given the space. The domestic hatcheries tend to concentrate their efforts on the production of the ever popular Moor, which is a black Globe Eye.

The finnage of the Globe Eye is similar to that found in the Oranda. If the fish has a very short body then the fins tend to be shorter than those found on the longer bodied fish. The paired tail fins in the very short bodied fish should be held well spread, being higher than they are long.

Globe Eyes come in every

This black Moor is blind; note the completely clouded cornea. Healthy in other respects, the fish can still find food.

color and scale type found in goldfish.

Although normal eyed black goldfish do exist, the Moor is the only truly solid dependably black goldfish, and this black color seems to be genetically linked to the Globe Eye gene. A Moor (black Globe Eye) should be solid black over its entire body. The fins should be black with no clear areas. Calico (nacreous) and metallic Globe Eyes should have bright rich well defined colors.

The Globe Eye is a hardy breed, but to do its best it should only be kept in an aquarium or pond that is free of sharp items that can damage this poor sighted but beautiful goldfish. Globe Eyes do not compete well with normal eyed goldfish, being very near sighted. It should only be kept with their own kind, or other breeds with vision problems (Celestials, Bubble Eyes, etc.).

Offspring of a cross between a Ranchu and an Oranda. Breed characteristics of either parent are not evident. Its headgrowth is minimal and a highly arched back is not present.

Mixed Breed Characteristic Goldfish: There are many more breeds of goldfish than those just listed, but those listed are considered to be the basic fancy goldfish breeds. Many of these basic breeds have at least one breed characteristic that is unique to that breed only, making them pure breeds for that type of breed characteristic.

There are other goldfish breeds with unique breed characteristics such as the Tosakin, Jikin, Nankin, Maruko (egg fish), Shukin and the recently developed Humanishiki, just to mention a few. Although some of these breeds are imported into America and England now and then, their numbers are very small, and they are so rare that even the most avid goldfish collectors, with great connections, will not be able to find some of them in their lifetimes.

Goldfish that have more than one breed characteristic (mixed breed characteristic or mixed trait goldfish) push the number of goldfish breeds available to the goldfish hobbyist up into the hundreds, with the possible combinations of breed characteristics going up into the thousands. Mixed breed characteristic goldfish such as the Pom Pom Oranda are fairly common (for rare breeds), while others like the Veiltail Pearlscale Oranda are extremely rare. Many mixed trait breeds are only a quickly passing breed which comes and goes over a two or three year period, while others have been around for hundreds of years.

For the goldfish breeder who has the patience to spend years line breeding, it is possible to take any of the basic breeds and combine them into a single unique mixed characteristic breed goldfish all their own. Given the massive variety in the goldfish genetic make up, it would be highly unlikely that any two breeders would be able to duplicate the other's mixed trait goldfish exactly.

Over the years I have owned two or more very different types of Bubble Eye Orandas, Pom Pom Globe Eyes, Lionheads, and given the fact that in Japan there are over 30 different breeds of Ranchus, I think you can see that if you have the time and patience you can develop your own unique breed of goldfish. All it takes is time.

This mixing of basic breed characteristics into one goldfish breed is not a job for the novice, as it takes years of dedicated work, and literally dozens of aquariums to develop new goldfish breeds. Since nearly all goldfish breed characteristics are deviations from the normal

goldfish, most are recessive genetic traits that take at least two generations to bring back from an out-crossing. And if you're really serious about developing a new goldfish breed, you should carry at least two or more lines in order to maintain vigor and successfully combine mixed breed traits.

This type of breeding program takes many aquariums or ponds, and should only be undertaken after long study, much experience and a long term achievable goal has been put in place. You should start by reading a book about the genetics of aquarium fish.

The hobbyist should not go into this type of breeding program with making money as a goal. In most cases the hobbyist will not be able to sell any of his fish for several generations, as many recently out-crossed goldfish are really ugly and are

The majority of a spawn of Chinese Lionheads will lack headgrowths and have poor backs like this young male.

The ancient bronze color of this male Oranda makes this the only black goldfish that has a metallic shine; all other black goldfish are more or less lusterless.

only useful to the breeder because of the genetic traits that they carry.

Due to their uncertain genetic make up, mixed trait goldfish should not be sold to the retail pet goldfish market until they are well fixed. This may take as little as five years, but in most cases it will take many more, so at least for the first several years the only money the hobbyist can hope to receive from their breeding program is by selling off the thousands of excess goldfish to the feeder goldfish market. (Fish used as food for larger fish, especially Oscars.)

If you're lucky enough to have purchased some mixed breed characteristic goldfish and plan on breeding them, then you should not expect to get a large percentage of these mixed trait fish in each spawn. Since many mixed trait goldfish are not well fixed, only a few fish in each spawn many exhibit the desired traits. Add to this the problem that many breed characteristics are late in developing, and this means that the hobbyist will have to raise a very large portion of each spawn until they can be sure they are not culling desirable goldfish.

Raising or finding mixed trait goldfish is a very difficult area of the goldfish hobby. When found they are expensive, and when spawned they are rare within a spawn. But the joy and pleasure received from owning one of these rare breeds, or developing your own is well worth the effort, as many are unique and one of a kind.

Pond Care

The subject of pond construction, location, filtration, drainage and maintenance are subjects for a much larger book than this one. Since space is limited, I'll just briefly cover the subject of caring for goldfish in a pond environment, and let you go to your local library or petshop for books that cover pond construction and some of the other pond related subjects more fully.

Many goldfish breeds are only really at their best when kept in an outdoor environment, and for many hobbyists that means a small pond. Even though all goldfish breeds will look and grow better in an outside pond, many short round double tail breeds should only be kept in very small ponds (four feet by six feet is a good size). The reason for this is the short round bodies of these breeds will become long and thin if they are raised in a large pond.

Some of the better goldfish breeds for the ornamental pond are all of the single tail fin breeds, the Fantail, Fringetail, Ryukin, Ranchu, and Pom Pom. These breeds are usually good swimmers and can avoid most predators. Remember the double tail breeds can't compete well for food against the single tail

A colored diagram for a garden pond with a miniature waterfall. The pool is usually lined with a strong plastic sheet whose edge is hidden and secured by a row of stone slabs.

breeds, so for best results try not to mix the two in the same pond.

Predators are a problem whenever you keep goldfish outside. Animals like frogs, snakes, racoons, birds, insects, cats, dogs, and some children can clean a pond out in no time. If your pond is strictly for ornamental value, then I would limit the goldfish in that type of pond to the single tailed breeds.

If the pond is mainly for goldfish, then I would highly recommend that you cover the pond with a screen to prevent predator losses. In the screened pond almost any goldfish can be kept successfully, if the pond is fairly small. Large ponds encourage long bodies and in many double tail breeds this is not desirable.

The pond should be deep enough to prevent rapid temperature changes. Depending on your climate this could mean a depth of 12 to 24 inches. If your goldfish are going to stay in the pond year round, it must be deep enough to prevent it from freezing solid. In the winter at least two thirds of the total water volume should remain unfrozen to prevent oxygen starvation and water quality problems.

The pond should have partial shade for at least half of the day. If the pond receives too much sunshine the water will turn a dark green from too much algae. Dark green water can cause low oxygen levels during periods of low light (cloudy days and at night), and if the algae is too plentiful it can kill the goldfish.

A garden pond's water should be replaced partially, just as it is recommended for an aquarium. If a complete change of water is required, the fish should be removed temporarily until chlorine, if present, has escaped into the air.

A view in cross section of a pond constructed from a commercially manufactured plastic tub supported by a concrete platform above the ground. The same structure can be placed under the ground, too.

Shade can be provided to the goldfish in the pond by growing water lilies and other water plants. The pond itself can be shaded by locating it near a building, constructing a lathe house over it or positioning it so that large distant trees will provide some shade during the heat of the day.

Be advised that many leaves of trees and shrubs can be toxic if they fall or are blown into a pond, so locate your pond as far away as possible from trees and large shrubs. All leaves, toxic or not, can cause water pollution problems if allowed to gather in the pond. They should be removed with a net regularly if they find their way into the pond.

Water quality in the pond is just as important as it is in the aquarium. Don't overcrowd, try to keep the water cool by shading, use a pond filtration system if needed, make regular partial water changes and don't overfeed.

The pond goldfish will get a lot of its food from natural sources. Food like insects and algae are usually always available in a pond in limited amounts. The hobbyists should feed their pond goldfish very carefully. Due to the variable temperatures of the outdoor pond, it is very easy to overfeed goldfish in the pond, and any uneaten food will quickly pollute the water.

If you have space, time and money for a pond then by all means try your hand with one. Remember a permanent pond needs to be very carefully planned and constructed to be successful. But the initial time spent planning a pond will be repaid many times by a beautiful easy-to-care-for pond.

Goldfish Societies

An American Shubunkin, six months old, male. The color of the American Shubunkin should be selected for pure skyblues, pure reds, and jet blacks, in that order.

Goldfish Societies in the U.S. and Great Britain are dedicated to all goldfish in general.

In Asia it is a different story. In Japan there are over 50 goldfish societies that are dedicated to only one single breed of goldfish each. The majority of these single breed societies are dedicated to the Ranchu, and each society has its own variety, with their own standard. The Azuma and Tosakin each have their own societies, but are very small when compared to the Ranchu societies.

We Americans are not as active in goldfish culture as the Asians, but we do have one national society, the Goldfish Society of America. We also have several smaller local goldfish clubs that are usually located in the larger cities. Many of the larger local aquarium societies are now including goldfish classes in their shows, and several of the larger shows are sanctioned by the Goldfish Society of America.

Being a member of a Goldfish Society has many positive advantages.

One of the biggest pluses of joining a society dedicated to the goldfish is the availability of information that cannot be found in detail in any book. I found in writing this book that I had to take entire subjects that I could have written chapters on, and condense them into just a few sentences. I feel that these few short sentences have helped to make the goldfish hobbyist aware of a subject, and with a little common sense and experience, the hobbyist will do just fine. But by joining a local or national goldfish society you won't have to guess. You can contact, either by mail or phone, any number of experienced goldfish hobbyists who would be more than willing to help.

The Goldfish Society of America has in place a goldfish information network that has two or more experienced hobbyists who are willing to help in every time zone in the U.S.

An American Veiltail, one year old, unicolored, female. This goldfish will in all like-lyhood never change to orange.

Another advantage of joining a goldfish society is at times rare or high quality goldfish can be purchased through ads placed in their newsletters. Many of these goldfish, especially those rare breeds that are raised by American hobbyists, can only be found through these ads.

The Goldfish Society of America has been in the forefront in raising the popularity of the fancy goldfish through an active educational program, which has allowed even the new hobbyist the chance to successfully keep fancy goldfish. Fancy goldfish are not the easiest fish to keep; some are very difficult to keep. But thanks to the hard work of the Goldfish Society of America, many more people are enjoying fancy goldfish than ever before.

An American Veiltail, two years old, tricolored, female. The totally black eyes on a nacreous goldfish are not desirable.

Index

Suggested Reading

The following books by T.F.H. Publications are available at pet shops everywhere.

AQUARIUM PLANTS—by Dr. K. Rataj and T. Horeman.
ISBN 0-87666-455-9; TFH H-966, hardcover. 448 pages, 244 color photos, 124 black and white photos.

A complete volume dealing with aquatic plants, including those for the garden pond. Description and methods of propagation are discussed for each species of plant.

GOLDFISH GUIDE—by Dr. Yoshiichi Matsui.
ISBN 0-87666-545-8; TFH PL-2011
Hardcover. 256 pages, 100 color photos, 38 black and white photos, 14 line illustrations.

Contains information on all aspects of the goldfish; its history, types, biology, ecology, diseases, breeding and genetics, by a Japanese author with more than 50 years of academic and practical experience about goldfish.

GOLDFISH AND KOI IN YOUR HOME—by Dr. Herbert R. Axelrod and William Vorderwinkler.
ISBN 0-86622-041-0; TFH H-909
Hardcover. 224 pages, 160 color photos, 20 black and white photos.

Revised edition of a proven popular and useful book on two of the most-kept garden pond fish, the goldfish and the koi. Discusses all major goldfish varieties, breeding, health care.

KOI AND GARDEN POOLS—by Dr. Herbert R. Axelrod
ISBN 0-86622-398-3, TFH CO-040, Hardcover; ISBN 0-86622-399-1, TFH CO-040S, Softcover. 128 pages, all photos and illustrations in full color.

Introductory, yet complete, book for anyone ready to keep koi in a garden pool. All aspects about pools and koi covered.

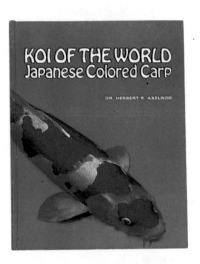

KOI OF THE WORLD—by Dr. Herbert R. Axelrod
ISBN 0-87666-092-8; TFH H-947, Hardcover. 239 pages, 327 color photos, 22 black and white photos.

Everything a garden pond keeper would like to know about the koi is in this book: varieties of koi, their needs, breeding, disease, cultivation in Japan.